D1570533

THE SLAVE NARRATIVES OF TEXAS

"Sugar Harvest in Louisiana and Texas" by Franz Hölzlhuber, ca. 1860.
Courtesy of the Glenbow Collection, Calgary, Alberta, Canada.

THE
SLAVE NARRATIVES
OF TEXAS

EDITED BY
RON TYLER &
LAWRENCE R. MURPHY

1997   STATE HOUSE PRESS   AUSTIN, TEXAS

FOR PAULA

Library of Congress Cataloging-in-Publication Data

The slave narratives of Texas / edited by Ron Tyler,
Lawrence R. Murphy.
p. cm.
Originally published: Austin, Texas. : Encino Press, 1974.
Includes bibliographical references.
ISBN 1-880510-35-9 (hc : alk. paper)
ISBN 1-880510-36-7 (pbk : alk. paper)
1. Slaves—Texas—Biography.
2. Afro-Americans—Texas—Interviews.
3. Afro-Americans—Texas—History—Sources.
4. Texas—Biography. I. Tyler, Ronnie C., 1941-
II. Murphy, Lawrence R., 1942-

E445.T47S52 1997
305.5'67'0922764—dc21   97-21615
[B]

Printed in the United States of America

cover design by David Timmons

COVER ILLUSTRATION:
"Sugar Harvest in Louisiana and Texas" from the painting by
Franz Hölzlhuber in the Glenbow Collection,
Calgary, Alberta, Canada.

All photographs courtesy of The Library of Congress

STATE HOUSE PRESS
P.O. Box 15247
Austin, Texas 78761

PREFACE

From the moment that Stephen F. Austin's original colonists brought Negro slaves into what was then a Mexican territory, politicians and historians have maintained that the slaves were well-treated in Texas. This belief stemmed from a legend which, in the words of the former City Superintendent of Public Instruction in Marshall, held that the slave "was provided by his master with a comfortable cabin and all the necessities of life. When he got sick the 'old master' sent for the best physician in the neighborhood . . . . This I assert was the *usual* treatment by the negroes at the hands of 'old master.' Anyone . . . old enough to recollect anything about ante-bellum times" could verify the statement, he claimed.[1]

Originally intended as a defense of slavery, this view was based on the arguments of planters, who were defending their very way of life from assault by crusading abolitionists. It was nurtured by later apologists who hoped to prevent the Negro from achieving full freedom or equality, and exists even today in a recognizable although altered form.

This legend probably emerged from the decades following the Civil War when former slave owners, who had just undergone what they considered to be a harsh period of Reconstruction, reflected on the prosperity of the pre-war years. As they reminisced, nostalgia clouded their thoughts. They repressed memories of brutal punishment, forced labor, and meager food, and emphasized instead the "jollyfications" of the slaves during the holidays.[2] Those who believe that everything in Texas is unique and others who insist that Texas is not a part of the "Old South" (and point to the "difference" in slavery to verify their claim) later compared Texas to the other southern states and reached a further conclusion. "Our" slaves not only were well-treated and happy, but they were better cared for and happier than those in other states, they asserted. Most of the early settlers were poor and owned only a few slaves. The colonists, therefore, treated their slaves better because they realized the value of the property. Had they mistreated their slaves, this reasoning continued, the Negroes would have run off, for West Texas was a desert through which no Negro could be successfully tracked, and Mexico, a land of freedom just like Canada, lay only across the Rio Grande.

This view completely overlooks the realities of slavery. Proponents of the argument neglect to point out that the colonists feared a slave uprising almost from the moment they arrived in Texas, and that an unsuccessful one did occur in 1836.[3] They ignore the fact that slaves did run off, and that hundreds, probably thousands of them sought refuge in Mexico. Presumably the Negroes were not fleeing from happiness.

Following the Civil War the legend took refuge in segregation. Those believing it convinced themselves that Negroes stayed apart by choice, that they preferred living in substandard sections of town and attending inferior schools, and that they had no interest in voting. Today the legend takes the form of moderation: Texas is a moderate state on the issues of civil rights for blacks, school integration, and housing. The implication seems to be that, since we are moderate—not like those rabid southerners—then we can move slowly to institute the changes the Supreme Court says we must. The legend has remained intact. Although it has assumed another form today, its historical shell remains unpenetrated. We still read that Texas blacks were better off than slaves in other states; in fact, that they were often better cared for than the master's own family![4]

Who is to say the legend is completely false? Usually a legend must contain some element of truth to endure so long and be so widely believed by blacks as well as whites. And there are many factors contributing to the character of the state, some of them capable of rendering slavery and the ensuing black-white relationship more humane. One might have been the emotional factor, which Professor Henry Allen Bullock has described in his writings.[5] Not the least of them is the geographical location of the state. The fact that slaves could escape to Mexico might have prevented some masters from mistreating their charges to the point of driving them to flight. The progressive Enlightenment philosophy inherited in some parts of the state may also have militated against a strict black-white division in society. Both Mexicans and Indians had to be considered. Probably more significant was the trend toward democracy that Frederick Jackson Turner identified in all the frontier states, for Texas was indeed on the frontier for decades. But as far as slavery was concerned it was also a part of the South.

In fact, the truth of the legend can probably never be completely affirmed or denied, but at least in the Slave Narratives we hear the testimony of a heretofore silent source, the Negroes themselves. Today the question of whether slaves in Texas were better treated than those in other parts of the country no longer seems important; no one has ever offered convincing evidence to prove that slaves anywhere preferred bondage to freedom. The testimony in the Slave Narratives points to the conclusion that has been a part of Western civilization ever since the ancients tried to divine the spirit of man. Western philosophy holds basically that man is created in God's image, that he possesses a free spirit, and that this spirit cannot be restrained, no matter how pleasurable (perhaps it would be better to say, how uncruel) the limitations. The theme of hundreds of myths, legends, and contemporary novels is that man cannot endure if his spirit is enslaved. We accept this as true for a Negro bondsman as well as a Madison Avenue executive. Therein lies the ultimate cruelty of slavery. Not only was the body held captive, but the spirit was also in slavery. It is time that we quit deceiving ourselves and document the history of the institution as historians, for in solving current racial problems, myths and self-deception are obstacles rather than aids.

When J. Frank Dobie said, "Never let facts stand in the way of truth," he pin-pointed the problem in dealing with slavery. In this case, the "facts" were set down by wealthy, slaveholding, conservative white planters and their apologists—or by propagandizing, humanistically oriented and equally uncompromising white abolitionists. One of the most insurmountable obstacles in writing about slavery, then, is overcoming the obvious prejudice, pro or con, of almost all the source material.

One form this prejudice took was that Negroes simply were not mentioned in the documents. They were not considered worthy of inclusion in the private correspondence or diaries of many of the planters, except in unusual cases—usually some instance concerning economics, such as buying or selling a slave or making a crop, or some humorous or human incident. Even those masters who kept diaries seldom noted that they did or did not whip their slaves or that the Negroes worked sixteen hours on such and such a day. The abolitionists, on the other hand, emphasized only the worst aspects of bondage, with cruelty stories getting more barbaric with each retelling. The positions were so far apart one would not expect either side to acknowledge the other's point of view. Most slave owners concealed any thoughts they might have had as to the unjustness of slavery, and abolitionists did not publicize cases of kind treatment of Negroes. It is particularly difficult in this case to fulfill the ideal role of the historian as defined by Professor Eugene C. Barker, longtime head of the history department at the University of Texas, who studied the early years of slavery in Texas so carefully: to gather all the pertinent evidence possible on both sides of the issue, then present an unbiased, honest, and, as best as can be determined, truthful analysis of slavery. Slaves did not keep diaries.

The best material the ex-slaves left is the Slave Narratives collection. Motivation to gather this information came from several sources. While white historians have concerned themselves with the scarcity of source material on black history only recently, Negro scholars observed the need much earlier. During the 1930's historian John B. Cade of Southern University developed an almost wholly neglected source. As he traveled through the rural South, he conceived of interviewing ex-slaves. Conducted largely by his students, the initial study appeared in 1935.[6] Cade later moved to Prairie View State College, where he gathered some 400 additional interviews.[7] Fiske University in Nashville carried out a similar program in Tennessee and Kentucky.[8]

Encouraged by these examples, Lawrence D. Reddick of Kentucky State College suggested to Harry Hopkins and other New Deal administrators that the federal government undertake such a program. A pilot program was initiated along the Ohio River.[9] With that experience, an expanded program covering almost the entire South was organized under the Federal Writers' Project of the Works Progress Administration. The principal task of the WPA authors was to prepare a series of guides on each state, but John A. Lomax, a Mississippi born white and an expert in the field of folklore, influenced the Writers' Project to include interviews with former slaves in its work.[10] By late 1936 a proposal to interview all available ex-slaves had been approved, and the necessary instructions sent to the various state officials.[11]

Lomax prepared a set of instructions for all the interviewers, listing a series of topics which might be covered in the conversations. The list included names and dates of birth, descriptions of life in the quarters and at work, food, clothing, treatment by overseers, Civil War experiences, the coming of freedom, contact with the Ku Klux Klan, and many more.[12] He suggested that these were only the starting point, adding that "the main purpose of these detailed and homely questions is to get the Negro interested in talking about the days of slavery. If he will talk freely, he should be encouraged to say what he pleases without reference to the questions."[13] The Texas interviews were then written up and sent to J. Frank Davis, the head of the state Writers' Project, who employed a man to edit them and, perhaps, rewrite the narratives. A similar process occurred in Washington, where Henry G. Alsberg, National Director of the Writers' Project, Lomax, or Chief of Negro Affairs Stanley Brown reviewed most of the stories.[14]

The results were enthusiastically received in Washington. No statewide plan assured complete coverage or random sampling, but industrious employees in Marshall, Fort Worth, and San Antonio collected large numbers of interviews, while fewer came in from more populous areas such as Dallas and Houston. The Texas project included 308 interviews. Only Arkansas accumulated more.[15] After reading the first dozen reports, Alsberg pronounced them "fine material."[16] Upon receipt of the final group of manuscripts, he congratulated Davis on the "excellence" of the collection, saying that the interviews were extremely "well written up."[17]

In dealing with the Slave Narratives, a problem that historians are just beginning to recognize surfaces: the problem of the interview. Oral history is a newly developing form of source gathering, and many questions immediately come to mind. Did the former slaves tell the truth? As Martin Jackson described it, securing honest, forthright information could be difficult. "Lots of old slaves closes the door before they tell the truth about their days of slavery," he warned. "When the door is open, they tell how kind their masters was and how rosy it all was."[18] Did the Negroes tell only what they thought the white interviewers wanted to hear?[19] In other words, did the questioner, by virtue of being white, involuntarily intimidate the Negroes and influence their answers. The fact that a government employee was in the home of a former slave, who probably depended on some form of government relief, might have had an effect.

Since the government employees were untrained in both oral history procedures and in the history of slavery, did they make the correct interpretations once they had the slaves' responses? Some editing was done, both in San Antonio, the state headquarters, and in Washington. Just how much it is impossible to say, but the narratives are much too consistent in form and content to have been prepared by a number of individuals working independently of each other. If the editors excluded information that did not conform to the contemporary view of slavery, much important material could have been omitted.[20] These questions must be weighed heavily with regard to the Slave Narratives, for the white interviewers understandably could have prejudiced or mishandled the ex-slaves' answers. But this does not mean that the questions and answers should be ignored; it means merely that we must use them as we use all historical sources, with proper caution.

The Slave Narratives present further problems. All the accounts are first-hand, or at least seem to be. Some of the former slaves were so young at the time of the interview, however, they would have been only small children at the time of the Civil War. In the cases where these Negroes tell fascinating tales of slavery, they probably are repeating incidents told them by older slaves rather than relating their own experiences. There is also the possibility that they fabricated their own stories. Another question we must consider is, how were the interviewers able to take down the words of the ex-slaves so accurately? No electronic recording equipment was used. Did they take notes and later expand them, imitating the language of the Negroes as remembered? Today a standard practice in oral history is to submit a copy of the interview to the subject for approval or correction.

Doubtless this was not done with the ex-slaves in these interviews.

Despite all the problems—both those of the historian routinely plying his trade and those particular ones associated with the ex-slave interviews—there is significant value in the Slave Narratives. As history, they are practically all we have from the viewpoint of the Negro on the subject of slavery in Texas. In them, perhaps, the answers to some of the questions puzzling to white men might be found. Why, for example, would a slave risk his life by running away if he were better treated and happier than slaves elsewhere? If, indeed, the Texas slaves were treated better than those elsewhere, it seems certain that the planters and overseers failed to convince them of it. Just how were the slaves of Texas treated? What activities made up their day? What was their diet? Were they well cared for, as the white planter sources indicate? Or were they neglected when ill and punished just as brutally as their southern cousins, and as various travelers in Texas indicated? Perhaps the most important reason why historians have traditionally viewed slavery in Texas as more bearable than in other states is that there is no large body of primary source material from the slaves themselves available for rebuttal. It is easy to condemn the institution in Virginia or Alabama because there are literally volumes of published writings of fugitives who escaped from those states to Canada, where they could speak freely. The Slave Narratives are the only such collection that exists for Texas. The interviews are also valuable in literature and the study of folklore, for even though the mind of the white man probably intruded in them at some point and to an undetermined degree, the language and spirit of the Negro still survives.

The interviews comprise four typewritten volumes in the Rare Book Collection of the Library of Congress.[21] In editing them for publication, we, with few exceptions, have attempted to keep the original form of the narrative. One of the purposes of the project was to study the Negro dialect. In an effort to document the language, the interviewers attempted to spell the words phonetically. We have corrected most of the spellings for the purpose of improving the readability. Given the problems of interviewing, we feel that untrained, white interviewers could not have copied the pronunciation precisely; the original spellings would be of little value to linguists. For the same reason—readability—we have inserted a few simple words (the, and, if, but) when we felt clarity demanded it. Such additions have not substantially altered the form or intent of the narratives. The interviewer often would ask questions to prompt a forgetful or reluctant subject. When he wrote up the interview, however, he omitted the questions and put the conversation in the form of a first person narrative. Our guiding principle has been to render a clear, understandable text by making only those changes we felt necessary, and without violating the integrity of the narratives.

NOTES

[1]R. P. Littlejohn, "The Negro of the South," included with interview conducted at Marshall, Texas, Sept. 12, 1887, Transcript P–0 39, H. H. Bancroft Collection. Italics added.

[2]Ibid.

[3]B. J. White to Austin, Goliad, Oct. 17, 1835, in Eugene C. Barker (ed.), *The Austin Papers*, III, 190.

[4]See Rupert N. Richardson, *Texas: The Lone Star State*, 2nd ed. rev., p. 164, and Seymour V. Connor, *Texas, a History*, pp. 184–185. The statement that slaves were better off in Texas than in other states, which Richardson included in the second edition of his book, has been somewhat modified in the third edition (see Richardson, Ernest Wallace, and Adrian N. Anderson, *Texas: The Lone Star State*, 3rd ed. rev., pp. 160–161). Connor goes even further, saying that in some cases the slaves might have been better cared for than the master and his family. While this might be true in the absolute sense—that is, one master might have done so—certainly it was not the usual situation, most likely not even a common situation.

[5]Professor Bullock argued that, although the system of slavery was essentially closed—that the Negro was not recognized as individual according to the "chattel concept"—there were ways the slave could overcome the anonymity of the institution. He documented several ways in which the slave and the master developed "personal intimacy," which he called the "hidden passage" by which some slaves overcame the institution's emphasis upon class rather than the individual. He argued that slaves did make advances under bondage. The system was not as repressive as some would have you believe. See Bullock, "A Hidden Passage in the Slave Regime," in James C. Curtis and Lewis L. Gould (eds.), *The Black Experience in America; Selected Essays*, pp. 3–32.

[6]John B. Cade, "Out of the Mouths of Ex-Slaves," *Journal of Negro History*, XX (July, 1935), 294–337

[7]Norman R. Yetman, *Life Under the "Peculiar Institution": Selections from the Slave Narratives Collection*, p. 343.

[8]Ophelia Settle Egypt, J. Masuoka, and Charles S. Johnson, *Unwritten History of Slavery: Autobiographical Accounts of Negro Ex-Slaves*.

[9]William F. McDonald, *Federal Relief Administration and the Arts*, pp. 720–721; B. A. Botkin (ed.), *Lay My Burden Down: A Folk History of Slavery*, p. x.

[10]John A. Lomax, *Adventures of a Ballad Hunter*, pp. 2–40, 189.

[11]Yetman, *Life Under the "Peculiar Institution*," p.363.

[12]Botkin, *Lay My Burden Down*, p. ix.

[13]Quoted in McDonald, *Federal Relief Administration*, p. 721.

[14]Davis to Alsberg, San Antonio, Oct. 7, 1937, in Texas File, Correspondence Pertaining to Ex-Slave Studies; McDonald, *Federal Relief Administration*, p. 722; Yetman, *Life Under the "Peculiar Institution*," p. 344.

[15]Yetman, *Life Under the "Peculiar Institution*," p. 357. Louisiana failed to participate.

[16]Alsberg to Davis, Washington, July 9, 1937, in Texas File.

[17]Alsberg to Davis, Washington, Aug. 3, 1937, in Texas File.

[18]Interview of Martin Jackson, below, p. 15.

19Almost all the employees of the Writers' Project were white, although at least one Negro worked on the project, questioning former slaves along the Brazos River. See Allen F. Kifer, "The Negro Under the New Deal, 1933—1941," pp. 237—238.

20Stanley M. Elkins (*Slavery: A Problem in American Institutional and Intellectual Life*) attempted to explain the phenomenon that the planters and many travelers insisted they saw: happy slaves who, in many ways, acted like children—like the mythical character Sambo, the name Elkins adopted for the character he described. Rather than deny the existence of that character, as did many historians who concentrated on runaways, slave rebellions, and other forms of resistance to white control, Elkins sought to explain him. To do so he used the analogy of the concentration camp and the childlike regression suffered by thousands of inmates in that closed system. The theory is, of course, controversial and debatable, but it does view slavery from a different perspective.

21Federal Writers' Project, *Slave Narratives, A Folk History of Slavery in the United States from Interviews with Former Slaves.*

ACKNOWLEDGMENTS

An endeavor of this sort inevitably depends upon the assistance and co-operation of a number of people. We are particularly indebted to Mrs. Abigail Curlee Holbrook of Austin and to Mr. Bob Dalehite, former Archivist of the Rosenberg Library, for their suggestions, insights, and encouragement in the study of slavery in Texas. We were greatly aided in this pursuit by industrious librarians who gathered bundles of interlibrary loan material, especially Miss Lucille Neu, former librarian at Western Illinois University and now at East Texas State University, and Mrs. Nancy Wynne, librarian of the Amon Carter Museum of Western Art. Mrs. Margaret McLean, newspaper librarian of the Amon Carter Museum, also aided our search by contributing various items that she discovered in her own work.

We are also thankful for the help that various persons gave us with source materials and with the manuscript. Professor Frank Smyrl of East Texas State first called our attention to Jean Charles Houzeau's comments on the institution of slavery. Mrs. Paul Morris of Texas Christian University translated the Houzeau letters. Richard Corby of Western Illinois prepared the appendix including the personal information on each of the slaves. Bruce J. Dinges of Rice University helped with proofreading and selecting narratives and photographs. Professor Donald E. Worcester of Texas Christian University read the manuscript and offered valuable suggestions and criticisms, as did Mr. Kenton Alexander of Fort Worth. Aid in providing typing services and copying materials came from Professor Walter Olson, Dean of Arts and Sciences, and the University Research Fund of Western Illinois University.

Of course, we are responsible for the final results, but it would have been most difficult to achieve this end, and we would have strayed many times, without such help and encouragement.

R. T.
L. M.

CONTENTS

INTRODUCTION

Slavery has always been an institution that possessed positive economic features as well as damning moral qualities. Although the rhetoric of its defenders and the nostalgic reminiscences of the planters following the Civil War have obscured the arguments, slavery in Texas is no exception. The newly formed Mexican government, independent of Spain since 1821, tried hard to base its governmental principles on the enlightened thought of the eighteenth-century French Revolution, which celebrated the equality of man. Texas, on the other hand, was settled by Anglo-American farmers, who saw in the fertile bottom lands of the Brazos and Colorado rivers an opportunity to make their fortunes. Their direst necessity was a labor force sufficient to till the thousands of acres that were given to them just for their choosing to settle in Texas. The two sides of the dilemma did not always stand opposed, however, for men could believe philosophically in the equality and dignity of man, yet see the necessity for a large, enslaved labor force for their plantations. Some might have preferred free labor had it been available. "I am a slaveholder," wrote Colonel James Morgan, the well-known Galveston Bay farmer, "was bred in a slave holding County—am tired of slaves and slavery."[1]

This same divided loyalty possessed Stephen F. Austin, the man responsible for the first Anglo-American settlement in Texas. He believed that the institution was an economic necessity in order for his colony to succeed. Had he not realized that, James A. E. Phelps reminded him when he wrote on January 16, 1825, that "Nothing appears at present, to prevent a portion of our wealthy planters from emigrating immediately to the province of Texas but the uncertainty now prevailing with regard to the subject of slavery."[2] Yet Austin regarded slavery as a moral evil, "that curse of curses, and worst of reproaches . . . that unanswered and unanswerable, inconsistency of *free* and liberal republicans."[3] Especially did he consider it a handicap after he began to think of independence as a possible course for Texas. "Texas . . . could sustain a respectable standing unless it should enfeeble itself by the system of negro slavery," he wrote.[4] On another occasion: "The idea of seeing such a country as this overrun by a slave population almost makes me weep . . . . Slavery is now most positively prohibited by our Constitution and by a number of laws, and I do hope it may always be so."[5] Despite the view of slavery as evil and immoral, both Austin, who owned only a few slaves, and the Mexican officials in Coahuila y Texas, where slavery had been legally abolished, collaborated to ensure the institution for the Anglo-American colonies in Texas.[6] *"Texas must be a slave country,"* Austin eventually concluded. *"It is no longer a matter of doubt."*[7]

From the moment that Austin received confirmation of the grant that his father, Moses, had not been able to fulfill because of his death, slavery was an important issue. The original grant to Moses did not mention slavery. By the time Stephen reconfirmed it, however, a provision had been added granting an additional eighty acres of land for each slave owned by the immigrant. Austin returned to Texas under the impression that the grant was his, but the governor of Coahuila y Texas refused to allow the settlers to take possession of the land. Austin left immediately for Mexico City, where he spent more than a year lobbying for the passage of a bill that would allow him to settle his land with slaveholders. As finally passed, the article allowed slavery in Texas, but it stipulated that all children of slaves born in Texas would be free upon reaching age fourteen.[8]

There was no doubt in Austin's mind that the Mexican government was unalterably opposed to slavery. The congress that met in 1824 to draw up a new constitution for the republic, had overwhelmingly adopted a decree outlawing the odious slave trade and providing harsh penalties for anyone convicted of the offense. Any "commerce or traffic" in slaves was "forever prohibited" in Mexico, declared the framers of the decree of July 13, 1824. "Slaves that are introduced [into Mexico] . . . are free by virtue of the mere act of treading Mexican territory," they added. No mention of the slaves then in Texas was made, so the colonists interpreted the decree as applying only to the slave trade, not to individual slaveholders bringing in their own Negroes. The Mexican congress adjourned in December, 1824, without making any clarification.[9]

Austin realized that there still might be trouble on the issue with the Coahuila y Texas legislature. Benjamin R. Milam probably summed up Austin's fears with more grace then grammar when he warned Austin that "the manner in which the slave question is desided will be a grait objection to the American population and I fear will put a Suden stop to that population."[10] After the new constitution was adopted, Austin was given another charter which stipulated that he could continue to introduce colonists into Texas, but that they would have to abide by any future laws regarding slavery. He became worried when the legislature assembled in 1827, for he knew it would be overwhelmingly anti-slavery. His brother, James E. Brown Austin, and the Texas delegate, Baron Felipe Enrique Neri de Bastrop, worked tirelessly to secure approval of the institution of slavery in Texas. Besides claiming that Texas needed slaves to be successful economically, they used the same argument that was employed for centuries by those who would keep the Negro enslaved: they are not yet ready for freedom, they would become "*vagabonds* and rogues" if given their freedom abruptly. They needed to work under a good master and learn a trade before being released, the Texans argued. Surprisingly, the *Ayuntamiento* of San Antonio also came to the support of Austin's colony, claiming that slavery was an economic necessity and pointing out that the original 300 families, who had immigrated under Austin's first contract, would be deprived of their constitutional rights if their slaves were freed.[11]

The legislature apparently listened to these arguments, for when the constitution of 1827 was adopted it included an article which declared that all children born to slave parents would be free, but that slaves could be brought into Texas for six months following publication of the decree in the prinicpal cities of each department. Six months later the legislature set up rules by which this provision was to be enforced. Each municipality was to prepare a list of slaves within its jurisdiction; all deaths and births were to be reported every three months, and the municipality was to keep a careful register. Other decrees were issued, intended to make conditions more tolerable for those who would remain slaves for life. Each time ownership of slaves changed hands, which according to law could only be by inheritance, one-tenth of the Negroes would receive their freedom. Slaves could change masters if they could find someone to buy them, and municipalities were charged with the responsibility of providing the best available education for the freed children.[12] "The restrictions as to Slavery in this State present very material obstacles to the settlement of Texas by emigrants from the southern States," Austin admitted to Joel R. Poinsett in November, 1827.[13]

The biggest hurdle was yet to come—complete emancipation. President Vicente Guerrero issued the decree on September 15, 1829, stating that slavery was abolished, all Negroes were freed, and that the owners would be compensated at some future date.[14] Colonists and prospective settlers were shocked. "I doubt nott you have taken Measures to Surpress it," John Durst of Nacogdoches wrote Austin. "For Gods Sake advise me on the subject by the return of Mail we are ruined for ever Should this Measure be adopted."[15] R. R. Royall, about to move his family and slaves from Alabama, queried Samuel May Williams, Austin's secretary, "if the Slave Question Rests as it did when I was there, is it necessary to use any precaution in Introducing them?"[16] "The news of the President's decree abolishing slavery throughout the Mexican republic, occasioned, and still produces much excitement, among emigrants to our country," Ira Ingram wrote Williams from New Orleans in January, 1830. "Altho' I felt and expressed every confidence in the belief that it *would* not effect property taken to the country . . . I have not in every instance been able to inspire others with the same confidence . . . ."[17]

Austin took a rational approach to the matter, indicating that he had learned the methodology of the Mexican bureaucracy. "I will *not* violate my duty as a mexican citizen," he answered to Durst. Austin recommended that the colonists make their representations through official channels, stating that they had come to Texas believing that the guarantees made them at that time would be honored, and that the settlers had taken the oath to uphold the Mexican constitution because of these promises. He further suggested that the people point out that the state constitution specifically permitted introduction of slaves for six months after its proclamation, and that the people "*will* defend it, and with *it*, their property." Don Ramón Músquiz, the political chief in Bexar and a friend of Austin, also appealed to the president on Austin's behalf, and withheld publication of the decree in Texas until a decision had been reached. The governor of Coahuila y Texas also supported the colonists' position.[18]

On December 2, 1829, President Guerrero issued a decree exempting Texas from the general emancipation edict. Several reasons probably motivated his action: the practical inconvenience of carrying out the law, the economic upset that all the officials in Texas threatened would ensue, and, probably, his personal lack of commitment on the issue. Perhaps Guerrero also feared that the colonists would revolt if their appeal were not upheld. It would not have been the first time a state had rebelled against the federal government to protect its rights under the constitution as it understood them. The emancipation decree was not carried out in other states, for another was issued in April, 1837. Had all the slaves been freed in 1829 it would have been unnecessary to pass another decree in 1837.[19] Slavery, the controversial institution that doomed Texas to deny the equality of man and to participate in a disastrous struggle that destroyed untold life and property—the Civil War—also enabled the state to become a major cotton producer and was thus permitted a foothold.

Even if Guerrero had not exempted Texas, the colonists had devised a way to bring in additional slaves after the six months time limit specified in the constitution had expired. "Slaves cannot be introduced as slaves," Austin advised his brother-in-law, James F. Perry, "but as indented or hired servants."[20] Before coming to Texas, a slave owner would go before an official and declare that the bondsman wanted to go to Texas with his master. A document of indenture would be drawn up stating that upon entering Texas the Negro would become free, but that he would be obligated to the master until he had paid off the expense of the trip, his food and clothes used on the trip and during the period of indenture, and, on occasion, for instruction received from the master in certain subjects. Colonel James Morgan brought seventeen Negroes with him in 1831. Going before the secretary of the territory of Florida (who also happened to be the Mexican Vice-Consul), Morgan had his Negroes indentured to him for ninety-nine years. The men were "to learn the art and mystery of farming and planting," the women, "the art and mystery of cooking," or housekeeping, or sewing.[21] "The Constitution of Coahuila y Texas declares that 'nobody can be born a slave,' " summarized Colonel William F. Gray, a land company agent in Texas in 1836, " 'and the introduction of slaves under any pretext is prohibited.' But the law (some law or other) permits persons to bind themselves by contract to serve others for a term of years." Colonel Gray concluded that a large number of Negroes had been brought into the region. "I am told a great many are introduced there and held without that formality," he continued. "There is a general desire to hold slaves, and it is permitted by common consent, no one being willing to prosecute for the violation of the law."[22] In other words, the Anglo-Americans had gone to the system used all over Mexico—peonage. Despite their moral reservations, both Austin and the Mexican officials of Coahuila y Texas had finally fixed slavery on the colony.

The number of Negroes in Texas, a region well-suited agriculturally to slave labor, grew rapidly once the major legal restrictions had been removed. From five male and two female slaves, counted in San Antonio in 1819, the slave population grew to 182,566 in 1860. There were reportedly 443 slaves in Austin's colony in 1825. Juan N. Almonte, following his reconnaissance of Texas in 1834, estimated that there probably were 1,000 bondsmen in the region, but that perhaps was a conservative figure since he underestimated the white population by almost fifty per cent.[23] Because of the rebellion against Mexico in 1836 and the ensuing chaos in Texas, it is impossible to document the number of slaves in that year, but it has been estimated by various historians at approximately 5,000. The Texas consul in London, Arthur Ikin, calculated that there were some 11,323 slaves in the republic in 1840; the number for 1845 has been estimated at 23,624. The most accurate counts, of course, are those made in the official census reports of 1847, 1850, and 1860. The state numbered 38,753 slaves in 1847, and the United States census takers recorded 58,161 Negroes enslaved in the state in 1850 and 182,566 in 1860.[24]

Blacks entered Texas by several different means. The most common one, of course, was importation by the master upon immigration. Some colonists sold their slaves along with their other possessions when they decided to move to Texas, but because Texas was a newly developing area, prices were higher there than in the United States. Most of the settlers, therefore, took their Negroes with them when they moved. Edmund Andrews brought a number of slaves with him when he emigrated to Texas in 1831.[25] While in Galveston in 1840, Francis C. Sheridan, a British diplomat, met a settler who had just landed with a "gang of Slaves," apparently afraid that he might be apprehended for engaging in the slave trade, although all the Negroes were his.[26] Adolphus Stern noted in his diary that on each of two days in February, 1842, ninety or more Negroes were brought into the republic through Nacogdoches. "Hurrah for Texas!" he excitedly wrote, as he thought of the potential wealth the slaves meant for the young nation.[27] Frederick Law Olmsted, while touring Texas in 1854, met a group of immigrants, with some fifty slaves, headed for the Brazos to settle. Hundreds of slaves were brought to Texas during the latter years of the Civil War by masters who hoped to get their Negroes as far from the center of conflict as possible, yet remain in a slave area.[28]

A few settlers made special slave-buying trips back to the United States. Asa Hoxey journeyed from his home in Alabama to Virginia to buy slaves before departing for Texas in 1832. While on an eastern trip, Guy M. Bryan, Stephen F. Austin's nephew, took the opportunity to purchase more slaves.[29] A. V. Darby, who owned a plantation near Dangerfield in Titus County, traveled to New Orleans in March, 1857, to purchase slaves, buying a Negro named Jo. When Jo ran away Darby discovered what shrewder buyers had known for some time—that slaveholders frequently sold their most troublesome Negroes to New Orleans markets, realizing that even hard-to-handle slaves would be passed on to Texas, where slaves were in demand.[30]

Hundreds, perhaps thousands, of slaves came into Texas via the domestic slave trade. Although hazardous, the trade had much to commend it to certain planters in need of laborers for their plantations and to traders who realized that one successful shipment might earn as much as $50,000. Some well-known Texans engaged in the trade. Although Edward Hanrick of Montgomery, Alabama, regarded James W. Fannin as "Worth Nothing and perhaps as we say *Wuss* than Nothing," he gave Fannin a letter of introduction to aid him in his "negro Speculation." Fannin, who hoped to bring Negroes from Cuba to Texas, offered thirty-six slaves for sale on Caney Creek and the Brazos River in 1835, claiming that the money was needed to purchase war materials for the planned revolt against Mexico. Another trader, Monroe Edwards, who spent his last days in Sing Sing prison for swindling, teamed with a New Orleans adventurer to bring slaves into Texas and used the profit from the illicit commerce to purchase Chenango Plantation, in Brazoria County.[31]

Other Negroes entered the state by means of the outlawed international slave trade. Francis Sheridan concluded that "very little pains are taken to prevent" the "Piracy. During the time we lay off Galveston two vessels with Slaves from Martinique land[ed] their cargos in security, the one below Velasco & the other at the Sabine." Sheridan felt the trade was so entrenched that "the only way to check the trafficking of slaves either brought from the main or through the U. States into Texas wd be to recognize her, & encourage emigration by every means in your power." Sheridan felt this might work, because he believed the "climate & soil do not require the *constitution* of a Negro—& one hard working white man is worth two blacks." Thus immigration would render slavery and the slave trade unnecessary.[32]

While he was in the Republic, Colonel Gray saw some Negroes who had just been brought in from Cuba. "About fifty of those poor wretches" were "living out of doors, like cattle," he declared. They were young, ranging in age from ten to twenty-five years. "Boys and girls huddled together," he continued. "They are diminutive, feeble, spare, squalid, nasty, and beastly in their habits. Very few exhibit traits of intellect." Nor did they seem accustomed to working. Gray described one girl who "sat apart and held no converse with the crowd" because she belonged to another tribe. She stood on her "dignity." There was a teenage boy, a runt, whom Gray assumed to be a prince because "deference is shown him. He claims the prerogative of five wives and flogs them at his pleasure." Even under these horrible conditions, however, Gray found the Africans to be "cheerful." They "sing and dance of nights; wear caps and blankets; will not wear close clothes willingly; some go stark naked." But their primitive habits most revealed themselves when the master slaughtered a beef; "the Africans wrangled and fought for the garbage like dogs or vultures; they saved all the blood they could get, in gourds, and feed on it." The only thing Gray saw that restored order to the scene was an "old American negro [who] stood over the beef with a whip, and lashed them off like so many dogs to prevent their pulling the raw meat to pieces." Gray obviously was repulsed at the spectacle. "This is the nearest approach to cannibalism that I have ever seen," he concluded.[33]

Mrs. Dilue Harris, who moved to Texas with her family in 1833, described a group of Negroes that slave trader Ben Fort Smith had just landed on the coast, as being so weak from the crowded conditions on the ship that they could not travel. They were practically starved when they arrived and reacted identically to those that Gray had seen. "As soon as the beeves were skinned," recalled Mrs. Harris, "the negroes acted like dogs, they were so hungry. With the help of father and uncle, the white men kept them off till the meat was broiled, and then did not let them have as much as they could eat." The Negroes were so nearly naked that Mrs. Harris' mother "would not permit us children to go near them. They laughed and chattered like monkeys," commented Mrs. Harris. "They did not understand a word of English. All the men and boys in the neighborhood came to see the wild Africans."[34]

The slave trade might have been more extensive than most Texans realized or admitted. Francis Moore, Jr., editor of the *Telegraph and Texas Register,* declared in 1843 that only one cargo of slaves had landed on the Texas coast since the Revolution—and that one by an Englishman—but there is evidence that large cargoes might have been landed both before and after the editor's claim. Phillip C. Tucker, II, acting United States District Attorney in Galveston, thought he found evidence of huge shipments in 1857 and 1858. In those years the famous camels imported by Secretary of War Jefferson Davis for experimentation in West Texas arrived in Galveston. Tucker became suspicious of the vessels, and a search revealed that the ships were outfitted as slavers; they contained special decks equipped with leg and arm shackles under the main deck, but no Negroes. Since the slave decks showed recent use, Tucker speculated that the merchant had landed the Negroes at the mouth of the Brazos and sold most of them to Colonel James Love, who had a large plantation along the river.

While touring the South in 1863, Lieutenant Colonel Arthur J. L. Fremantle, of the Coldstream Guards in England, met a "character" named Captain Thomas B. Chubb, who had been arrested on suspicion of being involved in the slave trade. "I was afterwards told," related Fremantle, "that the slave trading escapade of which he was accused, consisted in his having hired a colored crew at Boston, and then coolly *selling* them at Galveston."[35]

With the price of slaves continuing to soar in the late 1850's, a number of Texas newspaper editors clamored for the re-opening of the slave trade. Hamilton Stuart, publisher and editor of the Galveston *Civilian,* was one of the most outspoken proponents of the trade, but other influential Texans joined him. Willard Richardson of the Galveston *News* also supported legalization of the trade. At the New Orleans commercial and slave trade conference in 1856 the Texas delegation voted to legalize the traffic; the Texans voted for similar resolutions at the conferences in 1857, 1858, and 1859. The slave trade was an issue in both the state and national elections of the late 1850's and led to almost violent debates, but no legislation was adopted regarding it before Texas seceded in 1861.[36]

Blacks also were brought into Texas by slave dealers, who either resided in the state and purchased slaves to import or lived in other states and made infrequent trips to Texas to sell their Negroes. In 1823 John Botts sold perhaps as many as thirty or forty Negroes in the Austin colony.[37] New Orleans merchants hoped to underwrite Thomas F. McKinney's plan to bring Negroes from the Crescent City to Texas. Durant H. Daves, of Greensboro, Alabama, who got Dr. Ashbel Smith to act as his agent in Texas, lost several hundred dollars on an extended trip to the Republic when Smith advised him that the time was ideal for selling Negroes. Daves was able to sell only a few.[38] Negro traders continued to come into the state even after local markets were developed, for an out-of-state trader named Blakely lost one of his slaves, who ran away, while he was traveling through East Texas in 1857. After the Civil War started, slaves grew so scarce in Texas that traders resorted to illegal methods to get Negroes into the state, where they could be sold for premium prices. Isaac N. Miller, of Fannin County, reportedly helped slaves escape from their masters in Missouri so he could bring them to the Texas market.[39]

In an effort to take advantage of the high prices for slaves, Louisiana dealers frequently advertised in Texas newspapers, hoping to encourage the Texas planters to purchase their Negroes in New Orleans or Shreveport. J. A. Beard and Company, Joseph Bruin, George Pitts, D. M. Matthews, James White, J. B. Rowley, and many others purchased advertising space in Texas newspapers. They had a surplus of Negroes because many plantations in the South were being broken up as the land wore out. Texas was one of the few remaining unsaturated markets. The slaves would be purchased in New Orleans by the planter's agent, then taken to Texas. Olmsted saw such a "gang of negroes," guarded by a white man and a "very large yellow mastiff." He concluded that they probably had been consigned to some planter in Texas by his New Orleans factor in partial payment of his crop.[40] George W. Featherstonhaugh, who visited a north Texas plantation in 1834-1835, perhaps made a more accurate prediction than he realized when he wrote that the "occupation of Texas by the Americans . . . will convert the old slave-holding part of the United States into a disgusting nursery for young slaves, because the *black crop* will produce more money to the proprietors than any other crop they can cultivate."[41]

As the market for slaves continued to increase, local dealers in Texas began to compete with the New Orleans merchants who had dominated the state market for years. There had been slave dealers in Texas since the Republic, but not until after statehood did they become numerous. R. J. Manning and S. A. Hammett formed a partnership in Houston in 1846. The following year White and Shattuck opened a business. In 1848, F. Scranton advertised that his marts in Houston, Galveston, and New Orleans, charged only two and one-half per cent commission to buy or sell a Negro.[42] In 1853 Colonel John W. Walker of Galveston advertised that he had "just received direct from Virginia and Maryland 50 negroes from ten to twenty-five years old—one of the most likely lots of negroes ever brought to this State." He claimed that he would continue "to have on hand a supply of men, women and children, sufficient for the Texas market, of the best kind at prices as low as they can be bought in New Orleans." A slave dealer who reportedly looked after the more humanitarian aspects of his business was Colonel John S. Sydnor of Galveston. Sydnor refused to sell a respected Galveston slave to an undesirable buyer.[43] Olmsted noted the presence of a "prominent slave-mart" in Houston, "which held a large lot of likely-looking negroes, waiting purchasers." Olmsted saw signs in shop windows and doors and on hotel columns: "A likely negro girl for sale." "Two negroes for sale." "Twenty negro boys for sale." C. L. McCarty, an auctioneer and slave dealer in Galveston, advertised individual Negroes for sale in 1860. By that year there were nine licensed auction houses in Texas, and two persons called themselves Negro traders.[44] Several more probably were unlicensed or refused to admit the true nature of their business.

The slave population also increased when some masters turned to breeding their Negroes in an effort to increase the number and quality of their slaves. Sometimes this took the form of forced marriage, a rather common occurrence in slaveholding areas. Mrs. Fannie White, a former Texas slave, recalled that, "the old master at times picked a wife for a man slave. At other times, he gave the Negro man the woman of his choice," but the essential thing was that he marry. Other times the process was more brutal. Mrs. Harriet Robinson, considered an "excellent breeder" when she was a slave in Texas, was sold several times, each time bringing a handsome price. Mrs. Mae Dee Moore, another ex-slave, recalled that Mrs. Robinson was always "well cared for, was never whipped; but was with a broken heart constantly because she was used for breeding, as a lower animal, and was constantly separated from her children." Mrs. Moore also remembered a slaveholder in Texas who "bred and raised his own slaves." He selected three or four "heavyweight men" and forced them to stay in a cabin with several women. "In this way," she concluded, "he bred his slaves as he did his stock. If one of these selected women did not breed, she was sent to do heavier work."[45]

Jean Charles Houzeau, a Belgian scholar in Texas to study geology, associated breeding with lasciviousness. Obviously hoping to incite public opinion against slavery in a series of letters published in the *Revue trimestrielle* in Brussels, he asserted that the white owners took advantage of the female slaves "in any way imaginable." Lamenting the loss of a healthy female slave who had run away, one planter, complained to Houzeau that his "one pretty mulatto, very well put together, too," seemed "to be sterile. Father and I just haven't been able to get her with child." Pointing out that the owners wanted "white" slaves because they were worth more when sold, Houzeau claimed that he had softened the man's words in translation, but that they had been spoken with an "ease and cold-bloodedness which he could have used in talking about his cows."[46]

Throughout the slavery era in Texas, wealth and success of the individual planter as well as the South as a whole undoubtedly were associated with possession of slaves. Following a trip to Texas, William Kennedy, who replaced Arthur Ikin as Texas consul in London, estimated that each "field negro" in Texas was worth $500 a year if he cultivated cotton, the market crop, and Indian corn, an important feed crop. Featherstonhaugh guessed that for every "working negro" the planter could reap six to eight bales of cotton.[47] Although probably exaggerated, these figures indicate the faith many whites, even those who opposed slavery such as Featherstonhaugh, placed in the system. Writing in the *Texas Almanac for 1858,* John Henry Brown claimed that the slave produced the "great staples" of cotton, sugar, rice, hemp, tobacco, coffee, "which cannot be grown either by white or free labor to meet the demands of the world."[48] In 1849 the editors of the *Texas Republican* warned their readers that, "If Texas anticipated a speedy development of her agricultural resources, with the success that has attended the other southern states, she must depend for the result upon the institutions that have produced those results among which that of slavery is chief." The point is more dramatically illustrated by Colonel Fremantle's observations in Galveston. There a rather strict moral code as well as good business sense required that wealthy mercantile families restrict the display of their wealth for fear of offending their less fortunate customers. The only way they could publicly display their love for fancy clothes was through their slaves, whom they dressed outlandishly for regular Sunday afternoon outings. They sometimes loaned the Negroes their carriages and riding horses.[49]

Colonel Jared Ellison Groce moved to Texas in 1821 with 100 Negro slaves. The eighty acres per slave that he received from the Mexican government, coupled with his regular grant, made him one of the wealthiest men and largest landholders in the colony. By 1825 he was shipping cotton to market in New Orleans. When Alphonse Dubois de Saligny, the French charge d'affaires in Texas, visited the plantation in 1840, Leonard Waller Groce, Jared's oldest son, owned 180 slaves on his "magnificent estate" described as being "the equal of the most beautiful plantations along the banks of the Mississippi."[50]

Once slavery had been fixed on Texas, proponents and apologists had to justify the evil system, because abolitionists and unionists had been attacking it in Texas since the Revolution. Benjamin Lundy, probably the foremost figure in the American anti-slavery movement before 1830, claimed that the entire rebellion against Mexico was part of a plot to admit another slave state into the Union.[51] Slaveholding Texans responded that they kept Negroes not only because it was economically necessary, but also because it was in harmony with natural law and the best system for the Negro. The most eloquent defenses of slavery were written by southerners whose essays appeared in such popular publications as *DeBow's Review* or the *Southern Cultivator,* but Texas had spokesmen just as articulate if not as original. "Slavery came to the Southern man authorized by the Supreme Law of the Land," claimed John S. ("Rip") Ford, physician, newspaper editor, and former Texas Ranger, who always took an unequivocal stand on slavery. "It came to him authorized by time, and custom, and law. The assumption in the Declaration of Independence that 'all men are created equal' was not intended to include the African race, or was a falsehood on its face. It was an institution sanctioned by the Bible, and it had all the authority of time to uphold it."[52]

On another occasion, Ford declared, "The Savior erected his standard in the very midst of thousands of bondsmen, and while rebuking every species of sin, never raised his voice against the legitimacy of the institution." He left no doubt as to his position: "The South has the Bible on their side. If there is any one institution by the Word of God, it is that of slavery."[53] The editor of the Austin *Southern Intelligencer* supported Ford's contentions with an article copied from a Georgia newspaper. Since the book of Revelation is considered to be prophetic, asserted the anonymous writer, those believing that slavery was doomed should consult the sixth chapter, fifteenth verse, which indicated that *"bond men"* would be living at the time of the Second Coming.[54] John Henry Brown, the state representative from Galveston, furthered this logic in an article he wrote for the *Texas Almanac* in 1857.

> The African is an inferior being, differently organized from the white man, with wool instead of hair on his head—with lungs, feet, joints, lips, nose and cranium so distinct as to indicate a different and inferior grade of being. Whether this comes from the original law of God, we will not here discuss. But the grim fact is as true as that man exists.[55]

In a resolution before the House of Representatives, Brown had assumed the "superior capacity of the white man in the descending scale to the black man" and that the "black man or negro, has shown himself to be a distinctively inferior intellectual being, incapable of self-elevation or moral improvement, as evidenced by the absence of a single fact to the contrary, on the continent of Africa." Brown asked that the federal government legalize the slave trade, so Texas would be assured of a continuing supply of black laborers.[56]

Other Texans were aware of the absurdity of such claims, yet recognized the economic necessity of slavery. "We are abstractly opposed to slavery," wrote James P. Newcomb, speaking for himself and his partner, J. M. West, editors of the *San Antonio Herald,* but "we look upon it as one of those evils that must be left to root itself out, which it will do, as soon as free labor becomes as cheap and reliable, and not until then."[57] Some of the observations seemed to contain the seeds of economic determinism. At the conclusion of his tour, Francis Sheridan lamented that, regardless of the morality of the situation, the "great demand for labor, the immense price it fetches, the poverty & covetousness of the proprietors all militate against the poor nigger, and I fear his leisure moments are few & his lashes frequent."[58] Despite what his personal feelings might have been, Governor Peter H. Bell echoed these sentiments in his 1849 address to the state legislature. "Texas occupies . . . an interesting position in the American Union," he told the lawmakers. "The large extent of territory embraced by her boundaries, a great portion of which is eminently adapted to the culture of cotton . . . will insure to her, at no distant day, a very large slave population . . . ."[59]

Another widely held justification for slavery was the contention that the climate in Texas, particularly along the river banks in the southeastern part of the state where most of the plantations were located, was too harsh for any white man to endure the hard work demanded to raise cotton or sugar. "It is the general opinion," related William Bollaert, who visited Texas to survey the gulf coast for the British admiralty, "that the low lands of the coast and a considerable distance inland can only be worked profitably by Negro labour, for the white men, even those of Mississippi and other southern states, cannot for any time stand continued exposure to the sun and miasma from the rich and wooded lands, which bring on agues, other fevers and great debility."[60] On the other hand, wrote Brown, "as a slave in a mild climate the negro is contented, cheerful, obedient and a long-lived laborer. He attains his highest civilization in slavery, receives religious instructions—becomes faithful, trustworthy and affectionate to his white master and superior."[61] Bollaert concluded that, "the Negro is but seldom attacked" with the same maladies that affect the white man.[62]

The fallacies of this argument should have been obvious to any keen observer. Several travelers specifically rejected the notion. "The climate of Texas from all I can learn," wrote Sheridan, "is in *the Interior* one of the healthiest under the sun." If that were not enough, the white men who worked beside the Negroes exposed the inaccuracy of the belief. Jean Charles Houzeau, who harbored zealous abolitionist tendencies, observed German settlers working in their own fields.[63] Olmsted visited a northern man who had two slaves and employed seven white hired hands. "He was well convinced from his experience," contended Olmsted, "that white men trained to labor could do more work, the summer through, than negroes."[64]

Olmsted's observations throughout the South led him to believe that a significant difference between slavery in Texas and in the other slaveholding states existed. In the South the institution was "accepted generally, as a natural, hereditary, established state of things," he wrote. "But in Texas, the state of war in which slavery arises, seems to continue in undertone to the present." " 'Damn 'em, give 'em hell,'—frequent expressions of the ruder planters towards their negroes, appeared to be used as if with a meaning—a threat to make their life infernal if they do not submit abjectly and constantly," said Olmsted. "There seemed to be the consciousness of a wrong relation and a determination to face conscience down, and continue it . . . ."[65]

Houzeau made a similar observation. He found some Texas planters to be civilized men: "The older and most respected families have conserved the restraint and courtesy handed down from father to son. They are hesitant to abuse the slaves and to mistreat poor whites." But, he continued, "for every large, old plantation of one or two hundred slaves, there are fifty small farms of ten or twenty slaves. These are the newly rich, the new slave masters who find pleasure in owning other men." With the coming of the Civil War, the "new rich," according to Houzeau, "lost all moral sense and political restraint." They were "interested in only one thing: *to make money.*"[66]

Houzeau's charges undoubtedly characterized only the harshest slaveholders, but likely pictured the attitude that all too frequently permitted barbarities under the auspices of slavery. Often the masters were described as being totally depraved human beings, who would go to any length to prevent [black] equality, but Frederick Olmsted found that to be an inaccurate generalization. In Austin he talked with "many cultivated, agreeable and talented persons; among them gentlemen whose manner of thinking on certain subjects, on which their opinions differed much from my own, greatly gratified me." Olmsted seemed surprised to learn that "these gentlemen . . . honestly and confidently" thought slavery to be a beneficial institution, "gradually and surely making the negroes a civilized and a Christian people, and paying its way (perhaps with handsome dividends) to the capitalists who are the stockholders." Olmsted also found that they believed that "all the cruelty, or most of it, is a necessary part of the process, necessary at least in the present constitution of property and society."[67]

Numerous observers pointed out that because the slaves were such valuable property, the masters treated them well. "Why shouldn't they?" insisted a former slave. "It was their money." For whatever reason, some slaveholders undoubtedly were kind to their Negroes. Former Governor Francis R. Lubbock recalled in his memoirs, for instance, that he had purchased a slave upon the Negro's request. The black had been the only slave on a farm nearby and was lonesome. He ran away and sent a message to Lubbock asking to be purchased. Lubbock made the necessary arrangements with the other planter, then sold the Negro his freedom and helped him purchase his wife and children from slavery.[68] David A. Warren attempted to buy a man from William Ballow, in San Augustine County, only to be turned down because the Negro was unwilling to leave his wife, and Ballow would not force him.[69] Several brief lines in personal correspondence testify to the relationship between masters and their slaves: "Remember me kindly to the negroes," James F. Perry wrote his son Stephen, while away from his Peach Point plantation.[70] Such a paternalistic feeling may have been common. Francis Sheridan concluded that "in the Towns" the blacks were "very kindly treated," but admitted that he could not pass judgment on the plantation slaves because he had not seen any of them.[71] William Bollaert reported that, "Generally speaking throughout the Republic the Negroes are well treated, and I can bear witness that they are not over-looked, or ill-used."[72]

The assertion is often made that slaves had medical care as good as, or perhaps better than, the master's family. Adolphus Sterne, a wealthy merchant, land agent, and jurist in Nacogdoches, frequently called the doctor to visit his sick slaves. In the papers of plantation owners a common document is the receipt from a doctor; one in the Perry Papers, for example, shows that the Perrys paid $20 for the doctor to visit a Negro man. When smallpox broke out among William H. Williams' slaves, he quickly called a doctor, who recommended that he separate the woman with the worst case from the other slaves. "He says the disease can be [c]hecked but the effect will never leave her," Williams lamented. Indicating why so many slaveholders were willing to spend money for a doctor's visit, he then added, "her value is very much reduced."[73]

There were those in Texas, however, who contended that the slaves were ill-treated. In an effort to make the Negroes bend to their will, reported General Manuel Mier y Terán, the masters "are making that yoke even heavier; they extract their teeth, set on the dogs to tear them in pieces, the most lenient being he who but flogs his slaves, until they are flayed."[74] Among the most descriptive of Houzeau's reports are the ones dealing with the treatment of the Negroes. "I have seen sick slaves and pregnant women whipped," he wrote. "I saw one slave in a plantation of Guadalupe, a mulatto, fall unconscious under the whip, and remained a long time between life and death." The pregnant Negro, whipped because she did not feel like working and forced by the master to go to the field anyway, gave birth to a stillborn child on the same day, then died herself. Houzeau described another Negro who was hanged by his arms. The slave reportedly died of hunger with a plate of freshly cooked meat sitting in front of him. A master Houzeau quoted regarding a runaway slave repeated a common story: "The scoundrel has never served us well. One hundred times my father has had to order me to whip him, and I took care to rub in spice and salt afterwards."[75]

One of the most barbarous scenes Houzeau described concerned the rental of a female slave. A German slaveholder named Von Lonz had gambled away so many of his possessions that he turned to renting his female slaves, Houzeau asserted. The "young girls," between fifteen and twenty years of age, "do well in the kitchen," are "well raised and educated, speak several languages, and have an attractive appearance," Von Lonz advertized. They could be hired by the month, week, or day. Von Lonz rented a young Negro named Amanda, "at the flower of adolescence . . . and practiced [in] the principles of Christian charity," to a particularly "common, vulgar man," who was a butcher by trade. Amanda was shocked. "I saw the girl fall down and hide her face in her hands," related Houzeau. " 'I cannot go,' " she cried. " 'I was born here, I have lived here, and here are my friends and sympathies. If I have done something wrong, punish me, master, punish me without restraint.' " Houzeau continued to describe the brutal scene: "Remembering her childhood, everything which reminded her of her dear home, the girl fell into praying and supplication. She soon lost all cognizance of what was happening to her." An older slave prepared her bag and Amanda was bodily forced into her new master's buggy. Houzeau left no doubt as to the man's intentions: "In the struggle, her hair became tangles and fell all across her face, which was covered with tears; her blouse was open slightly. This disorder brought covetuous and evil looks from the butcher. He sat with brutal joy beside his distraught companion, and whipped his horses harshly."[76] There is no way to check the veracity of Houzeau's account, which was intended for a European audience, but reports such as these hardly evoke the image of the contented slave.

George Fellows, a religious man and probably an abolitionist, complained bitterly to the Reverend Isaac Sawyer about conditions in Galveston. Fellows had recently been forced to explain to a master why he had listened to the complaint of one of the man's Negroes regarding her treatment. "I told him that servants were to be believed sometimes, as well as white folks," declared Fellows. A minister in Galveston, he continued, "can preach the truth plainly without fear if he does not touch slavery." Fellows advised Reverend Sawyer that Sawyer probably would not be welcome in this "slave holding world," because the local Baptist preacher was out of sympathy with his abolitionist tendencies—"you might catch him pursuing his slave with a badger club or a big stick."[77]

George W. Featherstonhaugh compared the treatment of the slaves to that of a horse. "The poor slaves I saw here did not appear to me to stand any higher in the scale of animal existence," he commented after visiting a north Texas plantation. "The horse does his daily task, eats his changeless provender, and at night is driven to his stable to be shut in." The following morning the horse is taken out for another day's work, Featherstonhaugh continued. "This is the history of the slave in Texas, differing in nothing from that of the horse, except that instead of maize and straw he is supplied with a little salt pork to his maize . . . ."[78]

Frederick Olmsted, of course, objected to the treatment of the Negroes.

He stayed for the night at a plantation near Victoria, where he "heard the master threaten his negroes with flogging, at least six times, before we went to bed." Both the planter and his wife apparently made a habit of cursing their slaves when anything went wrong. On another occasion, Olmsted visited an East Texas plantation, where he saw the eight year old son of the planter beating his puppy behind the house, and "swearing between the blows. His tone," said Olmsted, "was an evident imitation of his father's mode of dealing with his slaves."[79]

One of the most important unanswered questions about slavery in Texas concerns the daily life of the Negroes. Here the prejudice of the sources is most evident, with the masters and their defenders describing the humane care and the abolitionists emphasizing the horrors. A few ex-slaves had the opportunity to describe their treatment at the hands of various masters in interviews with historian John B. Cade and his students in the early 1930's. Mrs. Mae Dee Moore described a "very cruel" Harrison County slaveholder, who owned forty or fifty slaves and employed an overseer. "Slaves were beaten for the least offense," she claimed.

> Oftentimes when a slave was tied down and beaten almost to death, this man who weighed about one hundred and eighty-five or two hundred pounds, would get on the slave and walk up and down his back, stamping, occasionally saying, "if there is anything I like better than my drink, it is whipping a nigger." Many times he would have slaves whipped to death, have a hole dug and kick the dead slaves into it.[80]

Justice for most Negroes was little more than an abstract term. George Fellows recalled that in 1844 "a mob took a Negro from jail by force and hung him because some of the other citizens wanted him to have a fair trial by the course of law. Though a very bad Negro," Fellows admitted, "yet I doubt whether he intended the crime for which he was hung."[81] When a Negro named George was arrested in Nacogdoches in 1861, the citizens held a meeting to decide what to do with him. All present voted to condemn him to death for planning to burn the town. He was immediately hanged.[82]

The living conditions of the slaves were also bad. The Negroes had quarters of the "worst description, though as good as local custom requires," Olmsted noted. "They are but a rough inclosure of logs, ten feet square, without windows, covered by slabs of hewn wood four feet long. The great chinks are stopped with whatever has come to hand—a wad of cotton here, and a cornshuck there. The suffering from cold within them in such weather as we experienced, must be great."[83] On a well-regulated plantation, such as Jared Groce's, the slaves ate in large "eating halls," attached to the kitchen. Each family had its own house with a small plot of land behind it to raise a garden or some stock. Bollaert wrote that the slaves could sell the produce—pork and poultry—for their own benefit.[84] A Bowie County slave, Fannie White, reported that there were no kitchens in the slave quarters where she lived. "The cooking, if carried on at all in the cabins, was done in the big fireplace. The slaves ate and slept in the same room."[85]

While the food Negroes ate usually sustained life, as might be expected, it varied greatly depending upon the master and the position of the slave. Mrs. White said that the "food was weighed out weekly" on her plantation: "six pounds of meal, three pounds of meat and a little lard for a man and his wife." If the slave happened to be the master's cook, or was related to the cook, the fare was generally much better. The cook, according to Myrah Fisher, was "kindly treated and allowed to feed her children in the master's kitchen off such food as was left from the master's table." Mrs. Moore, however, described another master who "fed his Negroes on such poorly cooked food from troughs that they often ran away, [and he] had them chased down with bad blood hounds."[86]

The work of the slave in Texas was similar to and as hard as a Negro's work in any other part of the South. The attitude of some planters was characterized by Trasimon Landry, a slaveholder of French origin, who asked Houzeau why it should "matter to me if a slave lives only three years; in that interval he has been worth the price I had to pay."[87] Houzeau continued:

> This barbarous master extracted sixteen hours per day of forced labor from his blacks. He sounded the bell at 3 a. m. He whipped the foreman when the foreman did not sufficiently whip the blacks. They ate their meals in the field, beside their work tools. They were not permitted to rest or perform natural functions in private, for fear of wasted time. Work continued until 10 p. m., and many of the slaves, worn out, fell down asleep beside their tools and slept in the field without returning to their cabins at night.[88]

Houzeau's description probably is exaggerated, since he was striving for maximum effect on a European audience. If it is accurate, Landry was probably harsher than most masters.

On James F. Perry's Peach Point plantation, about ten miles from Brazoria, the Negroes were expected to cultivate cotton, corn, potatoes, and cane. In addition, they split rails for board and basket timber, tore down and built fences, dug ditches, shelled corn, killed hogs, scared the birds from the corn (usually work for the older slaves and the children), hauled wood, worked on the roads, repaired the house, killed beeves, and attended to the other farm animals. Their biggest jobs were cotton picking, plowing, and hoeing. Cultivation, harvesting, and conversion of sugar cane into molasses were among the most difficult jobs the Negroes had to perform.[89]

The work, of course, varied according to the type plantation or business the owner was engaged in. In discussing opening a saw mill, Austin M. Williams referred to slaves whom he classified as slab crosscut, pole crosscut, screw hands, choppers, teamsters, and job hands.[90] Many slaves were house servants, particularly in the larger towns such as Galveston. Others filled any one of several common occupations: cobbler, carpenter, blacksmith, seamstress, mechanic. Few of the plantations in Texas would have been considered self-sufficient, or a household factory, for that type of plantation, which has so permeated the popular image of the South, hardly existed in Texas, if indeed it ever really existed in the South.[91] Whatever the work of the slave in Texas, it primarily involved manual labor.

One of the most important aspects of slave life was religion. The slaves usually belonged to the same church as the master, with several of the Negroes preaching for their own black congregations. "The old master," related Fanny White, "would read the Negro Parson a chapter in the Bible, select his text, and give him some instructions about handling the subject." Olmsted told of a slave who defended his Baptist faith by asking, "you never read 'bout any *John de Methodis'*, did you?" The Negroes usually were given the opportunity each Sunday and Sunday night, and sometimes on Wednesday night, of gathering for prayer meetings, but, said Mrs. White, "they were not allowed to preach or sing loud for fear of disturbing their mistress." Often they got the remainder of Sunday off.[92]

Sometimes, rather than having their own service, which usually met in the slave quarters, the Negroes would be forced to attend church with the master. The white preacher would preach for the whites at the morning service and for the slaves in the evening. "He would use such expressions," claimed Mrs. Pricilla Owens, "as 'Don't steal your master's chickens,' 'Obey your masters,' 'Don't run away, don't lie.' " The master's cook, being well treated, attended church with the white people and, according to Myrah Fisher, "had churchgoing clothes as well as plenty of work clothes." In Galveston the slaves themselves built a Baptist and a Methodist church, with the assistance of the masters. The slave owners allowed the Negroes to hold a fair to raise money for their building.[93]

The stories of Negro celebrations are legendary. The Committee on Slaves and Slavery of the Texas House of Representatives asserted in 1857 that, "our slaves are the happiest . . . human beings on whom the sun shines."[94] To a large extent the stereotype of the "happy Negro" probably stemmed from recollections of festivals or celebrations, as well as from the nostalgia that gradually surrounded the whites' memories of the pre-war days as

Reconstruction was enforced throughout the South. William Bollaert described what might have been a typical holiday scene on December 31, 1843. The previous night a local store owner had permitted the slaves to have their Christmas party in his unfinished store. "It was late ere all arrived, many of them having had to come several miles," Bollaert reported. "It was a 'subscription' ball and the unfortunate Negro who could not raise a couple of bits . . . was not admitted to the commencement of the ball, but Black hearts wax soft and as midnight approached and the strains of music sweet, the excitement produced by dancing, the door keepers became benevolent and it was a public ball." It was a grand affair, with most of the slaves well dressed and behaved. "As the company arrived," continued Bollaert, "they were cordially greeted [with] bows and shaking of hands and introduced by the names of their masters and mistresses . . . ." When they danced, "every limb would be in movement, the truly joyous and hearty laugh would resound thru the room . . . ." They ate about midnight and continued dancing and celebrating until daybreak.[95]

Colonel Fremantle was quite surprised when he saw the usual Sunday afternoon leisure of the Galveston Negroes, who admittedly were in a different situation from the other Texas slaves; because Galveston is on an island, most of their work was that of a house servant rather than a field hand. "I saw innumerable Negroes and Negresses parading about the streets in the most outrageously grand costumes—silks, satins, crinolines, hats with feathers, lace mantles, &c., forming an absurd contrast to the simple dress of their mistresses," he related. "Many were driving their master's carriages, or riding on horses which are often lent to them on Sunday afternoons."[96]

If the master permitted, a slave marriage could also be quite an affair. Fanny White said that the couple usually would simply "jump over a broom together," but should the master decide that the slaves could "really marry," a feast would be arranged. "It was just some feast," related Mrs. White, "a hog, a cow, and everything . . . ."[97]

The whites frequently complained that the Negroes had too much leisure, particularly when rumors of an uprising or a scare had circulated. In 1854 the editor of the *Texas Monument* in LaGrange complained that "on Sundays and hollydays they are almost universally permitted to go anywhere without a special permit." The editor of the *Texas State Gazette*, John Marshall, warned that any gatherings were occasions for the slaves to discuss various incendiary plots. Sometimes the master saw fit to work the slaves on Sunday, and he often disbanded the weekly prayer gatherings.[98] "It was shown that the great rendezvous for bad negroes had been at the *"prayer meetings!"* claimed Marshall. "These meetings ostensibly held for a good purpose were the places where the negroes were seldom interfered with by the presence of the whites, and every kind of thievish plot, incendiary work, and conspiracy were concocted, circulated, discussed, and attempts made to mature them."99 As early as 1851, H. P. Brewster, then the editor of the *Gazette*, warned masters against the "incalculable" harm that would come from allowing slaves to hire their own time, while the editor of the *Texas Monument* reminded his readers that it was a crime to sell liquor to the slaves.100 The editor of the *San Antonio News* was insulted by the "impudent airs" which the slaves assumed when they walked the streets of the Alamo City in 1864, and called for more restraint by the slaveholders. The Negroes likely were aware that they would soon be free.101

Many slaveholders believed the slaves had too much free time because so many of them ran away or had opportunity to plot an escape attempt or an uprising. If the documents are to be believed, literally thousands of Texas Negroes either fled or participated in an organized attempt at rebellion.102 Even though southerners attempted to suppress news of insurrections, there are records of numerous rebellions or escapes. In 1828, General Mier y Terán noted that the "slaves are beginning to learn the favorable intent of the Mexican law toward their unfortunate condition and are becoming restless under their yoke . . . ."103

The first slave uprising in Texas occurred during the Revolution. The Texas leaders had feared such an event—in fact, Ben Milam had warned that Santa Anna intended to get the slaves to revolt—and Thomas Pilgrim asked Austin if there "would . . . not be great danger from the Negroes should a large Mexican force come so near."104 A few days after the skirmishing between the Texans and the Mexicans began, a large group of Negroes on the Brazos rebelled. More than 100 were captured and whipped, some were hanged. "The negroes . . . had devided all the cotton farms," wrote B. J. White to Austin, "and they intended to ship the cotton to New Orleans and make the white men serve them in turn."105

Rumors of slave uprisings precipitated tremendous unrest in 1856. In September the Vigilance Committee of Colorado County discovered a "well-organized and systematized plan for the murder of our entire white population, with the exception of the young ladies, who were to be taken captives, and made the wives of the diabolical murderers of their parents and friends." More than 400 Negroes reportedly were involved in the plot, which had as its motto, "Leave not a shadow behind." The slaves supposedly planned to flee to Mexico. Three "ring leaders" were executed within a few days of their capture. Other suspected revolts were uncovered in Lavaca, DeWitt, Victoria, Sabine, and Nacogdoches counties, probably as a direct result of the disturbance in Colorado County.106

The greatest rumor of slave revolt occurred in 1860, and greatly exaggerated accounts of suspected uprisings flew wildly about the state. Abolitionists were condemned for starting fires in Dallas and other cities, but it is nearly impossible to ascertain the truth of such reports because of the inaccurate reporting in the newspapers.[107] The following year Nacogdoches citizens hanged a Negro man they found guilty of planning to burn the town and incite a general insurrection of the slaves in the country. He had escaped, but several weeks later returned, because, according to a companion, " 'he had a purpose to accomplish.' " The investigators even found the "light wood" he had gathered to start the fire.[108]

Numerous slaves, who did not participate in large-scale uprisings, did run away from their masters, many of them trying to return to a favorite master or rejoin their family, but others seeking freedom in Mexico. Several Negroes who had fled from East Texas masters in 1841, caused particular alarm when a gang of fugitives killed two white men in the vicinity of the Lavaca River. A group of slaves escaped from plantations on the Brazos in 1843, causing various newspaper editors to call for more stringent controls over the Negroes. In 1844 the overseer of a Brazos River plantation was killed by a fleeing slave. The fugitive was shot that same day by a merchant who thought the slave was robbing him. In 1845 twenty-five Negroes stole horses and arms in Bastrop and ran away to Mexico. At least seventeen of them were soon captured, but slaveholders feared that the remaining eight succeeded in getting to Mexico. A Harrison County slave attacked his overseer with a knife and killed him while the overseer was administering a whipping to the Negro. However, other Negroes subdued the fugitive and turned him over to the master.[109]

In 1855 John S. Ford estimated that some 4,000 slaves worth more than $3,200,000 had escaped to Mexico. "Let men, goaded by frequent losses, once shoulder their rifles and make a forward movement in direction of the Rio Grande, and nothing short of success will satisfy them," he editorialized.[110] But the flights for freedom did not end with such threats; in fact, they increased as the Civil War approached, seeming to validate Frederick Olmsted's claim that "any great event having the slightest bearing upon the question of emancipation" caused unrest among the slaves.[111] Escapes became such a problem that even Sam Houston, who later repudiated the Confederacy and released his slaves in response to President Abraham Lincoln's Emancipation Proclamation, advocated a United States protectorate over Mexico. "It was humanity that prompted me," said Houston, who himself lost two slaves to Mexican freedom in 1842. "It was to give protection to Texas against the savage Indians . . . . It was to provide for the reclamation of our slaves who escape into her territory." Bondsmen continued to seek freedom with the number increasing significantly in 1864, after all but the "die-hards" admitted that the South had lost the war.[112]

Masters resorted to various methods to prevent the slaves from running away. The most common was whipping and other kinds of punishment. Fierce dogs were used to track the Negroes. Patrols were established throughout the state, and the editor of the *Texas Monument* urged his readers to make wider use of passes and "punish the master or overseer for suffering his slave to go at large without a special permit. It may be said that the foregoing plan is tainted with unnecessary cruelty," the editor admitted, but the system would not only redound to the interest of the master but would likewise be promotive of the happiness of the slave."[113]

Slaveholders in Texas had a further threat to hold over their Negroes—the Indian. A great deal of superstition surrounds the relationship between the Indian and the Negro, with some saying that the black feared that Indians would kill them on sight. The master, of course, encouraged that belief to keep the slaves under control. Other early residents of the state maintained variously that Indians were afraid of Negroes, that Indians always killed Negroes rather than take them captive, or that Indians never scalped Negroes. Blacks undoubtedly aroused much curiosity among the Indians. Captain Randolph B. Marcy wrote in 1866 that the Comanches killed slaves in order to send them to the "happy hunting grounds," where they would have a better life. On another occasion, Marcy described two Negro girls whom a trader had rescued from the Comanches. The girls were "shockingly scarred and mutilated" because the Indians had "scraped through their skin into the flesh, believing that beneath the cuticle the flesh was black like the color upon the exterior." As if that were not enough, the Comanches then "burned them with live coals to ascertain whether fire produced the same sensations of pain as with their own people, and tried various other experiments which were attended with most acute torture." After an intensive investigation of the relations between Negroes and Indians, historian Kenneth W. Porter concluded that the Indians basically viewed the blacks as a part of the white man's culture, but that some Negroes eventually won places in certain Indian tribes by virtue of exceptional enthusiasm or acts.[114]

Another threat to the safety of the master's property was the free Negro. The planters tried to remedy the problem by making it illegal for a free Negro to remain in Texas without specific approval of the legislature after September, 1836; but the law was widely disregarded. There were never many free Negroes in the state, but there are no accurate statistics. The census of 1850 showed 397; that of 1860, 355. But the records are not reliable, for sometimes Mexicans were counted as free Negroes, and free Negroes, who had gained the respect of the white community, were occasionally listed as white.[115] Regardless of the number of free Negroes in the state, slave owners continually blamed them for their troubles, for stirring up the slaves or encouraging them to run off. Often free Negroes were arrested on the suspicion that they might be fugitive slaves; other times they were simply arrested—for not obeying the law of September, 1836, and subsequent additions—and sold as slaves. In an effort to avoid the worst imaginable fate, some free Negroes indentured themselves to someone they hoped would make a good master. Free Negroes were considered fair prey by those who would befriend them, then sell them as slaves. If possible, free Negroes emigrated to Canada, for the fact that they could be denounced and claimed as a slave even in the free states, according to the Fugitive Slave Law of 1850, made their existence in the United States precarious.[116]

When General Robert E. Lee surrendered to General U. S. Grant, the commander of the United States forces, in April, 1865, the Civil War ended. In June, General Edmund Kirby Smith surrendered the Trans-Mississippi Department, which included Texas, and on June 17 Major General Gordon Granger assumed command of the District of Texas. Granger arrived in Galveston on June 19 and promptly issued an order freeing the Negroes: "The people of Texas are informed that . . . all the slaves are free," read General Order Number Three. "This involves an absolute equality of personal rights and rights of property between former masters and slaves, and the connection heretofore existing between them becomes that between employer and hired labor."[117] Many freedmen were unaware of the significance of the act, but most were overjoyed nonetheless. "Everybody went wild," recalled Felix Haywood. "We all felt like heroes, and nobody had made us that way but ourselves. We were free. Just like that, we were free."[118] One phase of a brutal era was over and another—Reconstruction—remained, but the slaves at least were free from bondage.

The question of whether slavery was economically profitable is often asked. Many express the belief that the institution was naturally dying by 1860. While this probably was true for the states of the old South, in Texas it was increasing. Ex-Governor Elisha M. Pease said in 1864 that he had thought slavery would last another half century in Texas. The states' economy was late in developing. Labor was scarce. Cotton production had increased from slightly more than 58,000 bales in 1849—1850 to well over 400,000 bales by 1860. After visiting Texas in 1839, Frédéric Gaillardet wrote that the republic's prosperity would continue for several years because of "the richness of the soil, the location at the southern end of the American Union, and, one must add, the toleration by the new constitution of slavery without restrictions and without limit." He reasoned that when the planters of the deep southern states tired of their worn out land and the attacks of the abolitionists, they would seek a "more hospitable country." "In the enjoyment of this position lies the germ of Texas's future greatness," predicted Gaillardet. "It will become, in the more or less distant future, the land of refuge for the American slaveholders; it will be the ally, the reserve force upon which they will rest . . . ."[119]

By 1861 Texans had begun to realize the truth of Gaillardet's claim. The increased number of slaves bore witness to the developing economy. Prior to 1830 the number of Negroes in Texas was insignificant. Following the establishment of the Republic in 1836, population grew at a rapid rate—an increase of 32.7 per cent from 1836 to 1847, the year of the first state census. The increase was 49.6 per cent from 1847 to 1850, and 179.73 per cent from 1850 to 1860. But the number of slaves grew at an even more astounding rate: 12.9 per cent from 1836 to 1847, 50 per cent from 1847 to 1850, and 213.8 per cent from 1850 to 1860. "It appears to us that people are going crazy," declared Robert W. Loughery of the *Texas Republican*, "for we cannot imagine any species of labor warranting such prices" as were being paid both for the purchase and the hire of Negroes. Even then the demand could not be met. Ironically enough, Texans were still buying slaves in the last months of the Civil War and advertising hundreds of dollars reward for the return of runaways in May, 1865.[120] The Civil War, then, seemed to catch Texas at the height of slave-induced prosperity. The eminent authority on slavery, George R. Woolfolk, has concluded that the institution was a profitable system in Texas when the question is asked in functional terms, that is, "whether wealth could be produced and exchanged creatively," rather than in terms of dollars and cents.[121]

The fact that a slave economy could function with apparent economic success, however, does not answer the arguments of many who have sought to prove that slavery would have had a bleak future had it been allowed to run its course. Indeed, Eugene D. Genovese, in his seminal study of the southern economy concluded that it had already exhausted itself before the Civil War. Inefficiency of slave labor, soil depletion, and poor quality in both crops and livestock are some reasons for his contention. The slave system really was not even supplying its own needs, he argues, much less keeping pace with the dynamic industrial economy emerging in the North.[122]

Many Texans might have agreed with Genovese. Southerners, said John H. Reagan who served as Postmaster General of the Confederacy, realized that they had a particularly "bad inheritance" in Negro slavery and were concerned because "they did not see how they were to be relieved" of the problem. Reagan concluded that something would have been done—"numbers of slaveholders and others in the southern states questioned the policy of slavery; a few set their slaves free; others favored the colonization of the negro in Africa"—had not the abolitionists pressed the point so vigorously. Slavery permeated the entire intellectual, social, and economic structure of Texas and the South. In attacking it the abolitionists also struck at the very essence of southern life; and the proud planter class naturally jumped to its own defense, including the institution of slavery, which was not only the weakest point but also the foundation of the structure. After the "slavery agitation became sectional and political," said Reagan, there could be no compromise. For this reason Reagan considered slavery to be the main cause of the Civil War.[123]

Many well-known Texans were caught in this tragic dilemma. James Morgan, a successful planter and slaveholder, admitted that he had grown tired of the institution. William Pitt Ballinger of Galveston obviously was plagued with guilt feelings regarding his "free soil" tendencies as well as his ownership of slaves. He took refuge in the fact that he would have spoken out against the institution had he been given the opportunity. "My own conscience is clear," he confided to his diary on December 31, 1860. "I expected to be called on to speak the night of the first [secessionist?] meeting—If I had had opportunity to speak that night, and had borne, as I should have done, public earnest and strong testimony to my union senti- ments, & to my conviction of the recklessness by which we are being guided, I shd feel better satisfied with myself."[124]

Perhaps the most pathetic figure, however, is that of Stephen F. Austin. Inspired with the zeal and ability that enabled him to make his coloniza- tion scheme a success, he decided that slavery was necessary or all his efforts would be in vain. Yet he severely condemned the moral and human aspects of the institution. The Mexican officials who worked with him—from Presi- dent Guerrero, to the Coahuila y Texas legislature, to the department officials in San Antonio—seemed to have been caught in the same predica- ment. Professing the ideals of the Enlightenment, they supported what they considered to be best for the interests of the colony and approved slavery for Texas. As Ulrich B. Phillips, the pioneer historian of slavery, concluded, "Plantation slavery had in strictly business aspects at least as many draw- backs as it had attractions. But in the large it was less a business than a life; it made fewer fortunes than it made men."[125]

Whether the slaves in Texas were happy is really not a fair question, for to say they were is, in reality, little more than an ill-concealed attempt to defend an institution that is now universally condemned. Perhaps Texas Negroes were a bit better treated than blacks throughout the South— although that is doubtful because the testimony of the Negroes themselves gives graphic evidence to the contrary. The basic questions about slavery were, and still are, moral. Regardless of what white men thought about the institution, the slaves themselves must be heard. The *Slave Narratives of Texas* provide that opportunity. A former slave once expressed the thought by observing, "Tisn't he who has stood and looked on, that can tell you what slavery is,—'tis he who has endured."[126]

Ronnie C. Tyler

NOTES

[1]Morgan to Mrs. J. M. Storms, Jan. 26, 1844, quoted in William Ransom Hogan, *The Texas Republic: A Social and Economic History*, pp. 23–24.

[2]Phelps to Austin, Pinckneyville, Miss., Jan. 16, 1825, in Barker (ed.), *Austin Papers*, I, Pt. 2, 1020.

[3]Austin to Mary Austin Holley, Brazoria, Dec. 29, 1831, in ibid., II, 730.

[4]Austin to ———— , [Dec. 31, 1831?], in ibid., II, 731.

[5]Austin to Thomas F. Leaming, San Felipe de Austin, June 14, 1830, in ibid., II, 415.

[6]Austin to José Antonio Saucedo, [San Felipe de Austin, Aug. 7, 1826?], in ibid., I, Pt. 2, 1401; Austin to the State Congress, [San Felipe, Aug. 26, 1824?], in ibid., 1406; Austin to the *Ayuntamiento* of Bexar, [San Felipe, Aug. 26, 1824?], in ibid., 1422; Governor Juan Antonio Padilla's Opinion Concerning Slavery, Saltillo, Nov. 30, 1826, in ibid., 1523–1526.

[7]Austin to Mary Austin Holley, New Orleans, Aug. 21, 1835, in ibid., III, 101–102.

[8]Lester G. Bugbee, "Slavery in Early Texas, I," *Political Science Quarterly*, XIII (Sept., 1898), 390–394; Eugene C. Barker, *The Life of Stephen F. Austin, Founder of Texas, 1793–1836*, pp. 31, 40, 43–79.

[9]Bugbee, "Slavery in Early Texas, I," pp. 397–399.

[10]Milam to Austin, Natchitoches, Mar. 30, 1827, in Barker (ed.), *Austin Papers*, I, Pt. 2, 1622.

[11]Bugbee, "Slavery in Early Texas, I," pp. 402–405.

[12]Ibid., pp. 407–408.

[13]Austin to Poinsett, Saltillo, Nov. 3, 1827, in Barker (ed.), *Austin Papers*, I, Pt. 2, 1704.

[14]Bugbee, "Slavery in Early Texas, II," *Political Science Quarterly*, XIII (Dec., 1898), 648–649.

[15]Durst to Austin, Nacogdoches, Nov. 10, 1829, in Barker, (ed.), *Austin Papers*, II, 285.

[16]Royall to Williams, Tuscumbia, Ala., June 24, 1830, in Samuel May Williams Papers.

[17]Ingram to Williams, New Orleans, Jan. 11, 1830, in Williams Papers.

[18]Quotes in Austin to Durst, San Felipe de Austin, Nov. 17, 1829, in Barker (ed.), *Austin Papers*, II, 289; Bugbee, "Slavery in Early Texas, II," pp. 652–653.

[19]Bugbee, "Slavery in Early Texas, II," pp. 655–656, 659; Eugene C. Barker, *Mexico and Texas, 1821–1835*, p. 54.

[20]Austin to Perry, San Felipe de Austin, Jan. 3, 1830, in Barker (ed.), *Austin Papers*, II, 317.

[21]Document No. 31-0106, Apr. 30, 1831, in James Morgan Papers.

[22]William F. Gray, *From Virginia to Texas, 1835: Diary of Col. Wm. F. Gray, Giving Details of His Journey to Texas and Return in 1835–1836 and Second Journey to Texas in 1837*, p. 67.

[23]Abigail Curlee, "A Study of Texas Slave Plantations, 1822 to 1865," pp. 2,

5—6; Juan N. Almonte, "Statistical Report on Texas," trans. by C. E. Castañeda, *Southwestern Historical Quarterly*, XXVIII (Jan., 1925), 198.

[24] Curlee, "Texas Slave Plantations," pp. 20, 22.

[25] Andrews to Williams, Brazoria, Apr. 13, 1831, in Williams Papers.

[26] Francis C. Sheridan, *Galveston Island, or a Few Months off the Coast of Texas: The Journal of Francis C. Sheridan, 1839—1840*, ed. by Willis W. Pratt, p. 50.

[27] Archie P. McDonald (ed.), *Hurrah for Texas! The Diary of Adolphus Sterne, 1838—1851*, pp. 79—80.

[28] Frederick Law Olmsted, *A Journey Through Texas; or a Saddle-Trip on the Southwestern Frontier*, p. 88; Cade, "Out of the Mouths of Ex-Slaves," p. 328; Arthur James Lyon Fremantle, *The Fremantle Diary; Being the Journal of Lieutenant Colonel Arthur James Lyon Fremantle, Coldstream Guards, on His Three Months in the Southern States*, ed. by Walter Lord, pp. 63—65, 68.

[29] Asa Hoxey to Robert M. Williamson, Montgomery, Dec. 2, 1832, in "Notes "Notes and Fragments," *Quarterly of the Texas State Historical Association*, IX (Apr., 1906), 285; Bryan to Mrs. Emily M. Perry, New Haven, Conn., Apr. 25, 1851, in the James Franklin Perry, Stephen Samuel Perry, Sr., and James Franklin Perry, Jr., Papers.

[30] *Standard* (Clarksville), Oct. 24, 1857; Benjamin Drew, *The Refugee: A North-Side View of Slavery*, p. 199.

[31] Quote in Hanrick to Williams, Montgomery, Aug. 30, 1833, in Williams Papers; Eugene C. Barker, "The African Slave Trade in Texas," *Quarterly of the Texas State Historical Association*, VI (Oct., 1902), 152—155; Walter P. Webb and H. Bailey Carroll (eds.), *The Handbook of Texas*, I, 547.

[32] Sheridan, *Galveston Island*, pp. 89, 117.

[33] Gray, *From Virginia to Texas*, pp. 158—159.

[34] Quotes in "The Reminiscences of Mrs. Dilue Harris, I," *Quarterly of the Texas State Historical Association*, IV (Oct., 1900), 97—98; see also Webb and Carroll (eds.), *Handbook of Texas*, II, 621.

[35] *Telegraph and Texas Register* (Houston), July 5, 1843; Curlee, "Texas Slave Plantations," pp. 39—40; Webb and Carroll (eds.), *Handbook of Texas*, II, 85; quotes in Fremantle, *Diary*, p. 54.

[36] Earl W. Fornell, "Agitation in Texas for Reopening the Slave Trade," *Southwestern Historical Quarterly*, LX (Oct., 1956), 245—259.

[37] Botts to Austin, Alexandria, La., Sept. 14, 1824, in Barker (ed.), *Austin Papers*, I, Pt. 1, 895; Austin to _____ Martin, San Felipe de Austin, Sept. 14, 1832, in ibid., II, 861.

[38] Curlee, "Texas Slave Plantations," pp. 43—46.

[39] *Weekly Independent* (Belton), Sept. 12, 1857; *The Standard*, Oct. 19, 1861.

[40] Curlee, "Texas Slave Plantations," p. 47; *The Galveston Journal*, Sept. 9, 1853; quotes in Olmsted, *Journey Through Texas*, p. 240.

[41] George W. Featherstonhaugh, *Excursion Through the Slave States from Washington on the Potomac to the Frontier of Mexico; with Sketches of Popular Manners and Geological Notices*, II, 189.

[42] *Telegraph and Texas Register*, Jan. 11, Nov. 16, Dec. 7, 1846; Curlee, "Texas Slave Plantations," p. 49.

43*Weekly Jour..al* (Galveston), Mar. 4, 1853; Earl Wesley Fornell, *The Galveston Era: The Texas Crescent on the Eve of Secession*, pp. 115, 151.

44Quotes in Olmsted, *Journey Through Texas*, p. 363; see also *Daily Civilian* (Galveston), Nov. 21, 1860; Curlee, "Texas Slave Plantations," pp. 51—52.

45Cade, "Out of the Mouths of Ex-Slaves," pp. 303, 306—307.

46J. C. Houzeau, *La terreur blanche au Texas, et mon evasion*, pp. 27, 82—83.

47William Kennedy, *Texas: The Rise, Progress, and Prospects of the Republic of Texas*, II, 383; Featherstonhaugh, *Excursion Through the Slave States*, II, 187.

48J. H. B. [John Henry Brown], "African Slavery," *The Texas Alamanac for 1858*, pp. 132—133.

49Quotes in *Texas Republican* (Marshall), Aug. 3, 1849; see also Fremantle, *Diary*, pp. 116—117.

50Rosa Groce Bertleth, "Jared Ellison Groce," *Southwestern Historical Quarterly*, XX (Apr., 1917), 361; quotes in Dubois de Saligny to Louis Adolphe Thiers, LaGrange, July 17, 1840, in Nancy Nichols Barker (ed.), *The French Legation in Texas*, I, 153.

51Eugene C. Barker, "The Influence of Slavery in the Colonization of Texas," *Mississippi Valley Historical Review*, XI (June, 1924), 3—36; Merton L. Dillon, *Benjamin Lundy and the Struggle for Negro Freedom*, pp. 236—237.

52John S. Ford, *Rip Ford's Texas*, ed. by Stephen B. Oates, p. 313.

53Quoted in ibid., p. 314n.

54*Southern Intelligencer* (Austin), May 19, 1858.

55[Brown], "African Slavery," p. 132.

56Committee on Slaves and Slavery, Texas House of Representatives, *A Report and Treatise. Slavery and the Slavery Agitation*, p. 3.

57Quoted in Dale A. Somers, "James P. Newcomb: The Making of a Radical," *Southwestern Historical Quarterly*, LXXII (April, 1969), 452.

58Sheridan, *Galveston Island*, p. 89.

59Quoted in *Northern Standard* (Clarksville), Jan. 26, 1850.

60W. Eugene Hollon and Ruth Lapham Butler (eds.), *William Bollaert's Texas*, p. 272.

61[Brown], "African Slavery," p. 132.

62Hollon and Butler (eds.), *Bollaert's Texas*, p. 272.

63Quote in Sheridan, *Galveston Island*, p. 120; see also Houzeau, *La terreur blanche*, p. 4.

64Olmsted, *Journey Through Texas*, pp. 359—360.

65Ibid., p. 123.

66Houzeau, *La terreur blanche*, p. 4.

67Olmsted, *Journey Through Texas*, pp. 112—113.

68Quote in interview of Will Adams, below, p. 19; see also Francis Richard Lubbock, *Six Decades in Texas, or Memoirs of Francis Richard Lubbock, Governor of Texas in War-Time, 1861—63*, ed. by C. W. Raines, pp. 136—137. For the traditional version of treatment of the slaves, see Richardson, *Texas, the Lone Star State*, 2nd ed., rev., p. 164. Richardson, Wallace, and Anderson, *Texas, the Lone Star State*, 3rd ed., rev., p. 161, contains a modified version of the legend.

69Warren to Thomas B. Huling, San Augustine County, Mar. 8, 1854, in Thomas B. Huling Papers.

[70]James F. Perry to Stephen S. Perry, Biloxi, Aug. 25, 1853, in Perry Papers.

[71]Sheridan, *Galveston Island*, p. 89.

[72]Hollon and Butler (eds.), *Bollaert's Texas*, p. 271; Bullock, "A Hidden Passage in the Slave Regime," p. 11.

[73]McDonald (ed.), *Sterne Diary*, pp. 101, 195; bill from Drs. Stephens and Gautier for 1851, in Perry Papers; quote in Williams to Thomas Jefferson League, Dine [?] Craig, Feb. 4, 1864, in Williams Papers. For a very traditional view of care and treatment of the slaves, see Connor, *Texas, a History*, pp. 184—185.

[74]Quoted in Alleine Howren, "Causes and Origin of the Decree of April 6, 1830," *Southwestern Historical Quarterly*, XVI (April, 1913), 397—398.

[75]Houzeau, *La terreur blanche*, pp. 6, 26, 88.

[76]Ibid., pp. 6—11.

[77]Fellows to Sawyer, Galveston, Oct.—, 1844, in George Fellows Papers.

[78]Featherstonhaugh, *Excursion Through the Slave States*, II, 189.

[79]Olmsted, *Journey Through Texas*, pp. 92, 116—117, 242—243.

[80]Cade, "Out of the Mouths of Ex-Slaves," p. 317.

[81]Fellows to Sawyer, Galveston, Oct.—, 1844, in Fellows Papers.

[82]*Texas Republican*, Nov. 23, 1861.

[83]Olmsted, *Journey Through Texas*, pp. 66—67.

[84]Bertleth, "Jared Ellison Groce," pp. 361—362; Hollon and Butler (eds.), *Bollaert's Texas*, pp. 271—272.

[85]Cade, "Out of the Mouths of Ex-Slaves," p. 296.

[86]Ibid., pp. 300, 307, 312. For a contrasting description, see Bertleth, "Jared Ellison Groce," pp. 361—362. Slaves on the Groce plantation, wrote Mrs. Bertleth, had ham, bacon, hot biscuits and fresh steak!

[87]If the field slaves cost $800 to $1,300, a reasonable price during most of the 1850's, and if a slave earned as much as William Kennedy estimated—$500 per year—then Landry's assertion is, perhaps, feasible. However, the latter figure has been questioned by authorities. For prices on slaves, see Warren to Huling, San Augustine Co., Mar. 8, 1854, in Huling Papers; Guy M. Bryan to James F. Perry, Travis, Austin Co., Sept. 15, 1851, and Thomas C. Thompson to S. S. Perry, Caldwell, Sept. 20, 1855, in Perry Papers.

[88]Houzeau, *La terreur blanche*, p. 5.

[89]Abigail Curlee, "The History of a Texas Slave Plantation, 1861—63," *Southwestern Historical Quarterly*, XXVI (Oct., 1922), 95—104.

[90]Austin M. Williams to William H. Williams, Cedar Brake, Sept. 19, 1859, in Austin May Williams Papers.

[91]Curlee, "History of a Texas Slave Plantation," p. 114, says Peach Point was self-sustaining. Eugene D. Genovese, *The Political Economy of Slavery: Studies in the Economy and Society of the Slave South*, p. 51, says, on the other hand, that almost all the "self-sufficient" plantations hired out much of their work.

[92]*Texas State Times* (Austin), Mar. 14, 1857; quotes in Cade, "Out of the Mouths of Ex-Slaves," p. 327; and Olmsted, *Journey Through Texas*, p. 77.

[93]Quotes in Cade, "Out of the Mouths of Ex-Slaves," pp. 312, 328; see also Fornell, *Galveston Era*, p. 84.

[94]Committee on Slaves and Slavery, *A Report and Treatise*, p. 50.

[95]Kenneth M. Stampp, *The Peculiar Institution: Slavery in the Ante-Bellum South*, p. 322; Hollon and Butler (eds.), *Bollaert's Texas*, pp. 299—300.

[96]Fremantle, *Diary*, pp. 58—59.

[97]Cade, "Out of the Mouths of Ex-Slaves," pp. 303—304.

[98]*Texas State Gazette* (Austin), Mar. 14, 1857; Curlee, "History of a Texas Slave Plantation," p. 118; Olmsted, *Journey Through Texas*, p. 88; *Texas Monument* (LaGrange), Sept. 19, 1854.

[99]*Texas State Gazette*, Mar. 14, 1857.

[100]Ibid., Sept. 13, 1851; *Texas Monument*, May 19, 1852.

[101]*San Antonio News*, June 4, 1864.

[102]Wendell G. Addington, "Slave Insurrections in Texas," *Journal of Negro History*, XXXV (Oct., 1950), 408—434.

[103]Quoted in Howren, "Causes and Origin of the Decree of April 6, 1830," pp. 397—398.

[104]Milam to Francis W. Johnston, Punto Lampasos, July 5, 1835, and Thomas J. Pilgrim to Austin, Columbia, Oct. 6, 1835, in Barker (ed.), *Austin Papers*, III, 82—83, 162.

[105]White to Austin, Goliad, Oct. 17, 1835, in ibid., p. 190.

[106]Quoted in Addington, "Slave Insurrections," pp. 414—415, 417; see also *The Standard*, Sept. 27, Oct. 11, 1856; *Texas State Times*, Sept. 27, 1856, Jan. 17, 1857.

[107]Addington, "Slave Insurrections," pp. 419—429; William W. White, "The Texas Slave Insurrection of 1860," *Southwestern Historical Quarterly*, LII (Jan., 1949), 259—285.

[108]*Texas Republican*, Nov. 23, 1861.

[109]*The Morning Star* (Houston), Sept. 14, Oct. 7, 1841; July 10, 1843; Mar. 12, Apr. 9, 1844; Jan. 9, 16, 1845; *Texas State Gazette*, Jan. 17, 1857.

[110]*Texas State Times*, June 2, 1855.

[111]Olmsted, *Journey Through Texas*, p. 475.

[112]Speech on Thomas Jefferson Green, Aug. 1, 1854, and Speech Delivered at a Know-Nothing Mass Barbecue at Austin, Nov. 23, 1855, in Amelia W. Williams and Eugene C. Barker (eds.), *The Writings of Sam Houston, 1813—1863*, VI, 80, 214. Quote in *Campaign Chronicle* (Nacogdoches), July 12, 1859. See also Mrs. David Winningham, "Sam Houston and Slavery," *Texana*, III (Summer, 1965), 93—104. Judging from the number of advertisements appearing in the newspapers, the number of fugitive slaves increased throughout the 1860's, but jumped significantly in 1864. Perhaps one reason for it was the large number of slaves being brought to Texas from the deep South to escape the invading Union armies.

[113]*Texas Monument*, Sept. 19, 1854.

[114]Quotes in Randolph Barnes Marcy, *Thirty Years of Army Life on the Border*, pp. 55—56; see also Kenneth Wiggins Porter, "Negroes and Indians on the Texas Frontier, 1831—1876," *Journal of Negro History*, XLI (July and Oct., 1956), 185—214, 285—310, esp. 309—310.

[115]Andrew Forest Muir, "The Free Negro in Harris County, Texas," *Southwestern Historical Quarterly*, XLVI (Jan., 1943), 216.

[116]*Morning Star*, Apr. 10, 1839. There is probably more literature available for study on the free Negro in Texas than on slavery. Andrew Forest Muir and Harold Schoen have published thorough studies. For example, see Schoen, "The

Free Negro in the Republic of Texas," *Southwestern Historical Quarterly*, XXXIX (Apr., 1936), 292—308, XL (July, 1936), 26—34, (Oct., 1936), 85—113, (Jan., 1937), 169—199, (Apr., 1937), 267—289, and XLI (July, 1937), 83—108. See also Muir, "The Free Negro in Jefferson and Orange Counties, Texas," *Journal of Negro History*, XXXV (Apr., 1950), 183—206; "The Free Negro in Fort Bend County, Texas," *Journal of Negro History*, XXXII (Jan., 1948), 79—85, and "The Free Negro in Galveston County, Texas," *The Negro History Bulletin*, XXII (Dec., 1958), 68—70. See further, Earl W. Fornell, "The Abduction of Free Negroes and Slaves in Texas," *Southwestern Historical Quarterly*, LX (Jan., 1957), 369—380.

[117]General Orders, No. 3, Galveston, June 19, 1865, in *The War of the Rebellion: A Compilation of the Official Records of the Union and Confederate Armies,* Series I, Vol. XLVIII, Pt. 2, 929.

[118]Narrative of Felix Haygood, below, p. 113.

[119]Diary of William Pitt Ballinger, Nov. 18, 1862—Oct. 20, 1864, entry for June 8, 1864, p. 173; Frédéric Gaillardet, *Sketches of Early Texas and Louisiana,* trans. and intro. by James L. Shepherd III, p. 68.

[120]*The Texas Republican*, Jan. 14, 1854, May 12, 1865.

[121]George R. Woolfolk, "Cotton Capitalism and Slave Labor in Texas," *Southwestern Social Science Quarterly*, XXXVII (June, 1956), 52.

[122]Genovese, *The Political Economy of Slavery: Studies in the Economy and Society of the Slave South*, pp. 109, 112, 130.

[123]John H. Reagan, *Memoirs, with Special References to Secession and the Civil War*, pp. 93—94.

[124]Ballinger Diary, Jan. 1—Dec. 31, 1860, entry for Dec. 31, 1860, p. 141.

[125]Ulrich B. Phillips, *American Negro Slavery: A Survey of the Supply, Employment and Control of Negro Labor as Determined by the Plantation Regime*, p. 401.

[126]Statement by John Little, in Drew, *The Refugee*, p. 142.

THE SLAVE NARRATIVES OF TEXAS

 CHAPTER I

THE ROAD TO TEXAS

SILVIA KING

I know I was born in Morocco in Africa and was married and had
three children before I was stolen from my husband. I don't know
who it was who stole me, but they took me to France, to a place
called Bordeaux, and drugged me with some coffee, and when I
knew anything about it, I was in the bottom of a boat with a whole
lot of other niggers. It seemed like we were in that boat forever, but
we came to land, and I was put on the block and sold. I found out
afterwards from my white folks it was in New Orleans where the
block was, but I didn't know it then.

We were all chained, and they stripped all our clothes off, and
the folks who were going to buy us came around and felt us all over.
If any of the niggers didn't want to take their clothes off, the man
got a long, black whip and cut them up hard. I was sold to a planter
who had a big plantation in Fayette County, right here in Texas.

When Marse Jones saw me on the block, he said, "That's a whale
of a woman." I was scared and couldn't say anything, cause I couldn't
speak English. He bought some more slaves, and they chained us together and marched us up near LaGrange in Texas. Marse Jones had
gone ahead, and the overseer marched us. That was an awful time, because we were all chained up, and what one did all had to do. If one
drank out of the stream, we all drank; when one got tired or sick, the
rest had to drag and carry him. When we got to Texas, Marse Jones
raised the devil with that white man who had us on the march. He got
the doctor man and told the cook to feed us and let us rest up.

3

SPENCE JOHNSON

The nigger stealers stole me and my mammy out of the Choctaw Nation up in the Indian Territory when I was about three years old. Brother Knox, Sis Hannah, and my mammy and her two step-children were down on the river washing. The nigger stealers drove up in a big carriage and mammy just thought nothing, because the ford was near there, and people going on the road stopped to water their horses and rest awhile in the shade. By and by, a man coaxed the two biggest children into the carriage and gave them some kind of candy. Other children saw this and went too. Two other men were walking around smoking and getting closer to mammy all the time. When he could, the man in the carriage got the two big step-children in with him, and me and sis climbed in, too, to see how come. Then the man hollered, "Get the old one, and let's get away from here." With that the two big men grabbed mammy, and she fought and screeched and bit and cried; but they hit her on the head with something and dragged her in and threw her on the floor. The big children began to fight for mammy, but one of the men hit them hard and off they drove, with the horses under whip.

This was near a place called Boggy Depot. They went down the Red River, crossed the river, and on down in Louisiana to Shreveport. Down in Louisiana we were put on what they called the "block" and sold to the highest bidder. My mammy and her three children brought $3,000 flat. The step-children were sold to somebody else, but we were bought by Marse Riley Suratt who . . . had a big plantation . . . . The house was right on the Texas-Louisiana line.

JAMES BOYD

I was born in that Phantom Valley in the Indian Territory which is now called Oklahoma. We lived in an Indian hut. My pappy was Blue Bull Bird and mammy Nancy Will. She came to the Indian Territory with Santa Anna from Mississippi, and pappy was raised in the territory. I don't remember much about my folks, because I was stolen from them when I was a real little fellow. I was fishing in the Cherokee River, and a man named Sanford Wooldrige came by. You see, the white folks and the Indians had a fight about that day. I was on the river and I heard yelling and shooting and folks running, and I slipped into some brush right near. Then came the white man, and he said, "Everybody killed, nigger, and those Indians are going to kill you if they catch you. Come with me, and I won't allow them to hurt you." So I went with him.

He brought me to Texas, but I don't know just where, because I didn't know anything about that place.

4

NELSON DENSON

Marse Jim Denson had an easy living in Arkansas, but folks everywhere were coming to Texas, and he decided to throw in his fortunes.
It wasn't too long after that war with Mexico, and folks came in a
crowd to protect themselves against Indians and wild animals. The
wolves were the worst to smell cooking and sneak into camp, but
Indians came up and made the peace sign and had a pow wow with
the white folks. Marse got beads or cloth and traded for leather
britches and things.

I want to tell how we crossed the Red River on the Red River Raft.
Back in those days the Red River was nearly closed up by this timber
raft, and the big boats couldn't get up the river at all. We got a
little boat and a Caddo Indian to guide us. This Red River Raft they
said was centuries old. The driftwood floating down the river
stopped in the still waters and made a bunch of trees, and the dirt
accumulated, and broomstraws and willows and brush grew out
of this rich dirt that covered the driftwood. This raft grew about a
mile a year, and the oldest timber rotted and broke away, but
this was not fast enough to keep the river clear. We found bee trees
on the raft and had honey.

It was a long time after we came to Texas when the government
opened up the channel. That was in 1873 [1874]. Before that, a survey had been made and they found the raft was a hundred and twenty-
eight miles long. When we were on that raft, it was like a big swamp,
with trees and thick brush and the driftwood and logs all wedged up
tight between everything.

ELI DAVISON

Marse Davison had a good home in West Virginia, where I was born,
in Dunbar, but most of it belonged to his wife, and she was the boss
of him. He had a great many slaves, and one morning he got up and
divided all he had, and told his wife she could have half the slaves. Then
we loaded two wagons and he turned to his eldest son and the next
son and said, "You're going with me. Crawl on." Then he said to his
wife, "Elsie, you can have everything here, but I'm taking Eli and Alex
and these here two children." The other two gals and two boys he
left, and pulled out for Texas. It took us almost two years to get here,
and Marse Will never set eyes on the rest of his family any more, long
as he lived.

Marse never married any more. He'd say, "There ain't another
woman under the sun I'd let wear my name." He never said his wife's

name any more, but was always talking of those children he had left behind.

We got here and started to build a one-room log house for Marse and his two boys. My quarters was one of those covered wagons, till he traded me off.

He cried like a baby [when I was sold], and he said, "I hate to do that, but it's the only way I'll have anything to leave for my two boys." Looks like everything went against him when he came to Texas, and he took sick and died.

FRANCIS BLACK

I was born in Grand Bluff in Mississippi on old man Carlton's plantation, and I was stolen from my folks when I was a little gal, and I never saw them no more. We kids played in the big road there in Mississippi, and one day me and another gal were playing up and down the road, and three white men came along in a wagon. They grabbed us up and one of the men said, "Shut up, you nigger, or I'll kill you." I told him, "Kill me if you want to—you stole me from my folks."

Those men took us to New Orleans to the big slave market. I had long hair, and they cut it off like a boy and tried to sell me, but I told them men who looked at me that the men had cut my hair off and stolen me. The man who cut my hair off cursed me and said if I didn't hush he'd kill me, but he couldn't sell us at New Orleans and took us to Jefferson.

I never knew what they did with the other gal, but they sold me to Master Bill Tumlin, who ran a big livery stable in Jefferson, and I belonged to him till surrender.

MARIAH ROBINSON

I was born over in Georgia in that place called Monroe, and mammy was Lizzie Hill, cause her massa was Judge Hill . . . . Judge Hill's daughter, Miss Josephine, married Dr. Young's son, who lived in Cartersville, in Georgia, but he had moved to Texas. Then my missy gave me to Miss Josephine to come to Texas with her to keep her from the lonely hours and being sad so far away from home. We came by rail from Monroe to Social Circle and then boarded the boat *Sweet Home*. There were just two boats on the line, the *Sweet Home* and the *Katie Darling*.

We sailed down the Atlantic Ocean to New Orleans, myself and my Aunt Lizzie and Uncle Johns, all with Miss Josephine. When we got to New Orleans we rested and put up in the trader's office. Us slaves, I mean. This is the way of that. Our Massa Bob Young, he was a cotton buyer, and he had left Georgia without paying a cotton debt, and they held us for that.

6

Miss Josephine wired back to Georgia to Dr. Young, and he came and got us out. He came walking down the street with his gold-headed walking cane. We were upstairs in the trader's office. I saw him coming, and cried out, "Oh, yonder comes Massa Young." He looked up and shook his gold-headed walking stick at me and said, "Never mind, old boss will have you out in a few minutes." Then he got the hack as soon as we were out and sent us to the port, in order to catch the boat. We got on that boat and left that evening. Coming down the Mississippi and across the Gulf we saw no land for days and we went through the Gulf of Mexico and landed at the port, Galveston, and we came to Waco on the stagecoach.

SARAH ASHLEY

I was born in Mississippi and Master Henry Thomas bought us and brought us here. He was a speculator and bought up lots of niggers and sold them. Our family was separated. My two sisters and my papa were sold to a man in Georgia. Then they put me on a block and bid me off. That was in New Orleans, and I was scared and cried, but they put me up there anyway. First they took me to Georgia, and they didn't sell me for a long spell. Master Thomas traveled around and bought and sold niggers. We stayed in the speculator's grove a long time.

After a while Master Mose Davis came from Cold Springs in Texas and bought me. He was buying up little children for his children. That was about four years before the first [Civil] war.

WASH INGRAM

After pappy ran away, mammy died, and then one day the overseer herded up a big bunch of us niggers and drove us to Barnum's Trading Yard, down in Mississippi. That's a place where they sold and traded niggers just like stock. I cried when Capt. Wall sold me, cause that was one man that was good to his niggers. But he had too many slaves.

Cotton was selling at a good price then, and those slave buyers had plenty of money. We were sold to Jim Ingram of Carthage. He bought a big gang of slaves and refugeed part of them to Louisiana and part to Texas. We came to Texas in ox wagons. While we were on the way, we camped at Keachie, Louisiana, when a man came riding into camp and someone said to me, "Wash, there's your pappy." I didn't believe it, because pappy was working in a gold mine in Virginia. Some of the men told pappy his children were in camp and he came and found me and my brothers. Then he joined Master Ingram's slaves so he could be with his children.

ELIZA HOLMAN

I'll tell you how we came to Texas. The meals were cooked by the campfire, and after breakfast we started, and it was bump, bump, bump all day long. It was rocks and holes and mudholes, and it was streams and rivers to cross. We crossed one river, must have been the Mississippi, and drove on a big bridge and they floated that bridge right across that river.

Massa and missus argued all the way to Texas. She was scared most of the time, and he always said, "The Lord is guiding us." She said, "It is fools guiding, and a fool move to start." That's the way they talked all the way. And when we got in a mudhole, it was an argument again. She said, "This is some more of your Lord's calls." He said, "Hush, hush, woman. You're getting sacreligious." So we had to walk two miles for a man to get his yoke of oxen to pull us out of that mudhole, and when we were out, massa said, "Thank the Lord." And missus said, "Thank the men and the oxen."

Then one day we camped under a big tree, and when we woke in the morning, there were worms and worms and worms. Millions of them came out of that tree. Man, man what a mess. Massa said they're army worms and missus said, "Why aren't they in the army then?"

MARTHA SPENCE BUNTON

I remember how Massa Spence brought us to Texas in wagons, and the way we knew when we hit Texas was because massa began to talk about a norther. When that norther struck, all the weeds and leaves just started rolling. Us poor, ignorant niggers thought at first they were rabbits, because we'd never seen a rabbit then. Massa Spence rode his horse and missie Spence came along in the richer way, in a coach. The children walked mornings and the older folks walked afternoons.

AMOS CLARK

When I was still half-grown, Marse Bob traded me to Marse Ed Roseborough, and we came to Belton to live. We piled ox wagons high with bedding and clothes and such, and old Marse had his books in a special horsehair trunk, which the hide still had hair on. It had brass tacks trimming it up, and it was sure a fine trunk, and he said, "Amos, you black rascal, keep your eye on that trunk, and don't get it wet crossing the water and don't let no Indian get it." We had a sizeable drive of cattle and some sheep and pigs and chickens and ducks.

Marse and Missus found where they wanted the house and we got them axes out and in a few days there was a nice log house with two big rooms and a hall between them, almost as big as the rooms. We had been on the road about six weeks and Missus was sure proud of her new house. Then we made logs into houses for us and a big kitchen close to the big house. Then we built an office for old Marse and made chairs and beds and tables for everybody. Old Miss brought her bed and spindly, little table, and we made all the rest.

BETTY SIMMONS

When Massa Langford was ruined and they were going to take the store away from him, there was trouble, plenty of that. One day massa sent me down to his brother's place. I was there two days and then the missy told me to go to the fence. There were two white men in a buggy and one of them said, "I thought she was bigger that." Then he asked me, "Betty, can you cook?" I told him I had been a cook's helper two, three months, and he said, "You get dressed and come on down three miles to the other side of the post office." So I got my little bundle and when I got there he said, "Gal, you want to go about 26 miles and help cook at the boarding house." He tried to make me believe I wouldn't be gone a long time, but when I got in that buggy they told me Massa Langford had lost everything and he had to hide out his niggers to keep his creditors from getting them. Some of the niggers he hid in the woods, but he stole me from my sweet missy and sold me so some creditors couldn't get me.

When we got to the crossroads, there were the massa and a nigger man. That was another slave he was going to sell, and he hated to sell us so bad he couldn't look us in the eye. They put us niggers inside the buggy, so if the creditors came along they couldn't see us.

Finally those slave speculators put the nigger man and me on the train and took us to Memphis, and when we got there they took us to the nigger traders' yard. We got there at breakfast time and waited for the boat they called the *Ohio* to get there. The boat just ahead of the *Ohio*, old Captain's Fabra's boat, was destroyed and that delayed our boat two hours. When it came, there were 258 niggers out of those nigger yards in Memphis who got on this boat. They put the niggers upstairs and went down the river as far as Vicksburg, that was the place, and then we got off of the boat and got on the train again, and that time we went to New Orleans.

I was satisfied then that I had lost my people and was never going to see them any more in this world, and I never did. They had three big trader yards in New Orleans and I heard the traders say that town was 25 miles square. I didn't like it so well, cause I didn't like . . . that big river. We heard some of them say there's going to throw a long war, and we all wondered why they bought us if we were going to be set free. Some were still buying niggers every fall, and we thought it too funny they kept on filling up when they were going to be emptying out soon.

9

They had big sandbags and planks fixed around the nigger yards, and they had watchmen to keep them from running away in the swamp. Some of the niggers they had just picked up on the road; they stole them. They called them "wagon boy" and "wagon gal." They had one big mulatto boy they stole along the road that way, and his massa found out about him and came and got him and took him away. And a woman who was a seamstress, a man who knew her saw her in the pen, and he told her massa, and he came right down and got her. She sure was proud to get out. She was stolen from along the road, too. You see, if they could steal the niggers and sell them for good money, those traders could make plenty of money that way.

At last, Col. Fortescue, he bought me and kept me. He was a fighter in the Mexican War, and he came to New Orleans to buy his slaves. He took me up the Red River to Shreveport, and then by buggy to Liberty, in Texas.

The massa, when a place filled up, he always picked up and moved to a place where there weren't so many people. That's how come the Colonel first left Alabama and came to Texas, and to the place they called Beef Head then but call Grand Cane now.

WILLIAM HAMILTON

Who I am, how old I am, and where I was born I don't know. But Massa Buford told me how during the war a slave trader named William Hamilton came to Village Creek where Massa Buford lived. That trader was on his way south with my folks and a lot of other slaves, taking them somewhere to sell. He camped at Massa Buford's plantation and asked him, "Can I leave this little nigger here till I come back?" Massa Buford said, "Yes," and the trader said he'd be back in about three weeks, as soon as he sold all the salves. He must still be selling them, cause he never came back so far and there I am and my folks were taken on, and I was too little to remember them, so I never knew my pappy and mammy. Massa Buford said the trader came from Missouri, but if I was born there I don't know.

The only thing I remember about all that is that there was lots of crying when they took me away from my mammy. That's something I will never forget.

BETTY FARROW

About three years before the war, master sold his plantation to go to Texas. I remember the day we started in three covered wagons, all loaded. It was celebration day for us children. We traveled from daylight to dark, except to feed and rest the mules at noon. I don't recollect how long we were on the way, but it was a long time, and

10

it wasn't a celebration toward the last. After a while we came to Sherman, in Texas, to our new farm.

BEN SIMPSON

Boss, I was born in Georgia, in Norcross . . . . My father's name was Roger Stielszen, and my mother's name was Betty. Massa Earl Stielszen captured them in Africa and brought them to Georgia. He got killed and my sister and I went to his son. His son was a killer. He got in trouble in Georgia and got him two good-stepping horses and the covered wagon. Then he chained all his slaves around the necks and fastened the chains to the horses and made them walk all the way to Texas. My mother and my sister had to walk. Emma was my sister. Somewhere on the road it went to snowing, and massa wouldn't let us wrap anything round our feet. We had to sleep on the ground, too, in all that snow.

Massa had a great, long whip platted out of rawhide, and when one of the niggers fell behind or gave out, he hit him with that whip. It took the hide everytime he hit a nigger. Mother, she gave out on the way, about the line of Texas. Her feet got raw and bleeding, and her legs swelled plumb out of shape. Then massa, he just took out his gun and shot her, and whilst she lay dying he kicked her two, three times, and said, "Damn nigger that can't stand nothing." Boss, you know that man, he wouldn't bury mother, just left her laying where he shot her at. You know, then there wasn't any law against killing nigger slaves.

He came plumb to Austin through that snow. He took up farming and changed his name to Alex Simpson, and changed our names, too. He cut logs and built his home on the side of those mountains.

BILL HOMER

In the year of 1860 Missy Mary got married to Bill Johnson and at that wedding Massa Homer gave me and 49 other niggers to her for the wedding present. Massa Johnson's father gave him 50 niggers, too. They had a grand wedding. I helped take care of the horses, and they just kept a coming; I expect there were more than 100 people there, and they had lots of music and dancing and cats, and I expect, drinks, because we made peach brandy. You see, the massa had his own still.

After the wedding was over, they gave the couple the information. That's where this nigger comes in. I and the other niggers were lined up, all with the clean clothes on, and then the massa said, "To give my loving daughter a start, I give you these 50 niggers." Massa Bill's father did the same for his son, and there we were 100 niggers with a new massa.

They loaded 15 or 20 wagons and started for Texas. We traveled from daylight to dark, with most of the niggers walking. Of course, it was hard, but we enjoyed the trip. There was one nigger called Monk and he knew a song, and taught it to us, like this:

Walk, walk, you nigger, walk,
The road is dusty, the road is tough,
Dust in the eye, dust in the tuft;
Dust in the mouth, you can't talk.
Walk, you niggers, don't you balk.

Walk, Walk, you nigger, walk.
The road is dusty, the road is rough,
Walk till we reach there, walk or bust.
The road is long, but we'll be there by and by!

Now we were following behind the wagons, and we sang it to the slow steps of the ox. We didn't sing it many times till missy came and sat in the back of the wagon, facing us, and she began to beat the slow time and sing with us. That pleased Missy Mary to sing with us, and she laughed and laughed.

After about two weeks we came to a place near Caldwell in Texas, and there were buildings and land cleared, so we were soon settled.

MATTIE GILMORE

I remember when we came from Mobile to Texas. By the time we heard the Yankees were coming, they got all their gold together and Miss Jane called me and gave me a whole sack of pure gold and silver, and said bury it in the orchard. I sure was scared, but I did what she said. There was more gold in a big desk, and the Yankees pulled the top off that desk and got the gold. Miss Jane had a pretty gold ring on her finger and the captain yanked it off. I said, "Miss Jane, are they going to give it back?" All she said was "shut your mouth" and that's what I did.

That night they dug up the buried gold, and we left out. We just traveled at night and rested in the daytime. We were scared to make a fire. That was awful. All on the way to the Mississippi, we saw dead men lying everywhere, black and white.

While we were waiting to go across the Mississippi, a white man came up and asked Marse Barrow how many niggers he had, and counted us all. While we were waiting the guns began to go boom, boom, and you could hear all that noise, it was so close. When we got on the boat it flopped this way and that and scared me. I sure don't want to see any more days like that one with war and boats.

12

VAN MOORE

Mammy told me it was this way how come the Cunninghams and the McKinneys came to Texas. When war began most folks back in Virginia who owned slaves moved further South, and lots to Louisiana and Texas, cause they said the Yankees would never get that far, and they wouldn't have to free the slaves if they came way over here. Besides, there were so many slaves running away to the north, back there. Mammy said when they started for here in the wagons, white folks told the poor niggers, who were so ignorant they believed all the white folks told them, that where they were going the lakes were full of syrup and covered with batter cakes, and they wouldn't have to work so hard. They told them that so they didn't run away.

Well, mammy said they came to the lake that had round things on top of the water. Course, they were just leaves, but the niggers thought there was the lake with the syrup, and one ran to the edge and took a big swallow, and spit it out, and said "Whuf!" I reckon he thought that was funny syrup.

CAROLINE WRIGHT

One day I saw a lot of men, and I asked the missus what they were doing. She told me they came to fight in the war. The war got so bad that Mr. Bob told us we were all going to Texas. We all started out on Christmas Day of the first year of Lincoln's war. We went in ox wagons, and we had mules to ride.

On the trip to Texas, one evening a big storm came up, and Mr. Bob, he asked a man to let us use a big, empty house. They put me by the door to sleep, cause I was the lightest sleeper. Some time in the night, I woke up and there stood the biggest haunt I ever saw. He was ten feet high and had on a big beaver coat. I hollered to my pappy "Pappy, wake up, there's a haunt." Next morning we got up, and there was nothing out of place. No, ma'am, we didn't catch the haunt; a haunt just can't be caught.

Next morning we started again on our journey, and some time in March we reached Texas. They took us all across the Brazos on the ferryboat, just about where the suspension bridge is now.

William Moore, age 82

 **CHAPTER II**

MEMORIES OF MASSA

MARTIN JACKSON

Lot of old slaves close the door before they tell the truth about their
days of slavery. When the door is open, they tell how kind their masters were and how rosy it all was. You can't blame them for this
because they had plenty of early discipline, making them cautious
about saying anything uncomplimentary about their masters. I, myself, was in a little different position than most slaves and, as a
consequence, have no grudges or resentment. However, I can tell
you the life of the average slave was not rosy. They were dealt out
plenty of cruel suffering.

WILLIAM MOORE

Marse Tom has been dead a long time now. I believe he's in hell. Seems
like that's where he belongs. He was a terribly mean man and had an
indifferent mean wife. But he had the finest sweetest children the Lord
ever let live and breathe on this earth. They were so kind and sorrow-
ing over us slaves.

Some of them children used to read us little things out of papers
and books. We'd look at those papers and books like they were something mighty curious, but we'd better not let Marse Tom or his wife
know it.

Marse Tom was a fitty man for meanness. He just about had to
beat somebody every day to satisfy his craving. He had a big bullwhip
and he would stake a nigger on the ground and make another nigger
hold his head down with his mouth in the dirt and whip the nigger

till the blood ran out and reddened up on the ground. We little niggers stood around and saw it done. Then he told us, "Run to the kitchen and get some salt from Jane." That was my mammy, the cook. He'd sprinkle salt in the cut places and the skin jerked and quivered and the man slobbered and puked. Then his shirt stuck to his back a week or more.

My mammy had a terrible bad back once. I saw her trying to take the clothes off her back, and a woman said "What's the matter with your back?" It was raw and bloody, and she said Marse Tom had beat her with a handsaw with the teeth to her back. She died with the marks on her, the teeth holes going crosswise on her back. When I was grown, I asked her about it, and she said Marse Tom got mad at her cooking and grabbed her by the hair and drug her out of the house and grabbed the saw off the tool bench and whipped her . . . .

One day I was down in the hog pen and heard a loud agony scream-ing up to the house. When I got close, I saw Marse Tom had mammy tied to a tree with her clothes pulled down, and he was laying it on her with the bullwhip, and the blood was running down her eyes and off her back. I went crazy. I said, "Stop, Marse Tom," and he swung the whip and didn't reach me good, but it cut just the same. I saw Miss Mary standing in the cookhouse door. I ran around crazy like and saw a big rock, and I took it and threw it, and it caught Marse Tom in the skull, and he went down like a polled ox. Miss Mary came out and lifted her pa and helped him into the house and then came and helped me undo mammy. Mammy and me took to the woods for two, three months, I guess. My sisters met us and greased mammy's back and brought us victuals. Pretty soon they said it was safe for us to come in the cabin to eat at night, and they watched for Marse Tom.

One day Marse Tom's wife was in the yard, and she called me and said she had something for me. She kept her hand under her apron. She kept begging me to come up to her. She said, "Give me your hand." I reached out my hand, and she grabbed it and slipped a slip knot rope over it. I saw then that's what she had under her apron, and the other end tied to a little bush. I tried to get loose and ran around, and I tripped her up, and she fell and broke her arm. I got the rope off my arms and ran.

Mammy and I stayed hidden in the brush then. We saw Sam and Billie, and they told us they were fighting over us niggers. Then they told us the niggers had declared to Marse Tom that there weren't going to be no more beatings, and we could come up and stay in our cabin, and they'd see that Marse Tom didn't do anything. That's what mammy and I did. Sam and Billie were two of the biggest niggers on the place, and they had gotten the shotguns out of the

16

house some way or the other. One day Marse Tom was in a rocker on the porch, and Sam and Billie were standing by with the guns. We all saw five white men riding up. When they got near, Sam said to Marse Tom, "First white man who sets himself inside that rail fence gets it from the gun." Marse Tom waved the white men to go back, but they galloped right up to the fence and swung off their horses.

Marse Tom said, "Stay outside, gentlemen, please do. I've changed my mind." They said, "What's the matter here? We came to whip your niggers like you hired us to."

Marse Tom said, "I've changed my mind, but if you stay outside, I'll bring you the money."

They argued to come in, but Marse Tom out-talked them, and they said they'd go if he brought them three dollars apiece. He took them the money, and they went away.

Marse Tom cussed and rared, but the niggers just stayed in the woods and fooled away their time. They said it was no use to work for nothing all those days.

VAN MOORE

If old Missy Cunningham ain't in heaven right now, then there isn't any, cause she was so good to us we all loved her. She never took the whip to us, but I heard my mammy say she knew a slave woman owned by Massa Rickets, and she was working in the field, and she was heavy with child which was not yet born, and she had to sit down in the row to rest. She was having the misery and couldn't work good, and the boss man had a nigger dig a pit where her stomach fitted in and laid her down and tied her so she could not squirm around any, and flogged her till she lost her mind. Yes, sir, that's the truth; my mammy said she knew that woman a long time after that, and she was never right in the head again.

JACK CAUTHERN

My master was Dick Townes, and my folks came with him from Alabama. He owned a big plantation fifteen miles from Austin and worked lots of slaves. We had the best master in the whole county, and everybody called us "Townes' free niggers," he was so good to us, and we worked hard for him, raising cotton and corn and wheat and oats.

Most of the slaves lived in a two-room log cabin with dirt floors over in the quarters, but I lived in the master's yard. That's where I was born. There was a tall fence between the yard and the quarters, and the other nigger boys were so jealous of me they wouldn't let me cross that fence into the quarters. They told me I thought I was white, just for living in the master's yard.

17

Me and my young master had good times. He was near my age, and we'd steal chickens from old miss and go down in the orchard and barbecue them. One time she caught us and sure wore us out! She'd send us to pick peas, but few peas were picked!

Old miss was good to her colored folks. When she'd hear a baby crying in the night, she'd put on boots and take her lantern to go see about it. If we needed a doctor she'd send for old Dr. Rector, and when I had the measles she gave me some pills big as the end of my finger.

CAREY DAVENPORT

I was a sheep minder them days. The wolves were bad, but they never attacked me, because they'd rather get the sheep. Old Captain wanted me to train his boy to herd sheep, and one day young massa saw a sow with nine pigs and wanted me to catch them, and I wouldn't do it. He tried to beat me up, and when we got to the lot, he had a pine knot, and he caught me in the gate and hit me with that knot. Old Captain was sitting on the gallery, and he saw it all. When he heard the story he whipped the young master, and the old lady, she didn't like it.

One time after that she was sitting in the yard knitting, and she threw her knitting needle off and called me to come get it. I done forgot she wanted to whip me, and when I brung the needle she grabbed me, and I pulled away, but she held on to my shirt. I ran around and around, and she called her mother, and they caught and whipped me. My shirt just had one button on it, and I was pulling and gnawing on that button, and directly it came off, and the whole shirt pulled off, and I didn't have anything on but my skin. I ran and climbed up on the pole at the gate and sat there till master came. He said, "Carey, why are you sitting up there?" Then I told him about the whole transaction. I said, "Missus, she whipped me cause young marse John got whipped that time and not me." He made me get down and get up on his horse behind him and ride up to the big house. Old missus, she had gone to the house and gone to bed with her leg, because when she was whipping me she stuck my head between her knees, and when she did that I bit her.

WES BRADY

Grandpa Phil told me about meeting his massa. Massa Jeems had three or four places, and grandpa hadn't seen him, and he went to one of the other farms and met a man coming down the road. When the man said, "Who do you belong to?" Grandpa said, "Massa Jeems." The man said, "Is he a mean man?" Grandpa said, "I don't know him, but they say he's pretty tight." It was Massa Jeems talking, and he laughed and gave Grandpa Phil five dollars.

18

JACOB BRANCH

Old massa he was sure a good old man, but the old missy, she was a tornado. Her name was Miss Liza. She could be terrible mean. But sometimes she took her old morrel—that's a sack made to carry things in—and went out and came back with plenty of joints of sugar cane. She took a knife and sat on the gallery and peeled that cane and gave a joint to every one of the little children.

Mama, she worked in the big house, doing cooking and washing. Old massa bought a colored man named Uncle Charley Fenner. He was a good old colored man. Massa brought him to the quarters and said, "Renee, here's your husband," and then he turned to Uncle and said, "Charley, this is your woman." Then they were considered married. That was the way they married then, by the massa's word. Charley, he was a good step-pa to us.

HARRISON BECKETT

One time us boys got some watermelons out of the brush and hit them or dropped them to break them open. There came massa, and he caught us not working but eating his watermelons. He told my daddy to whip me. But lots of times when we were supposed to mind the calves, we were out eating watermelons in the brush. Then the calves got out, and master saw them run and caught us.

Old massa was kind and good, though. He had a partiality about him and wouldn't whip anybody without good cause. He whipped with the long, keen switch and it didn't bruise the back, but sure did sting. When he got real mad, he pulled up your shirt and whipped on the bare hide. One time he was whipping me and busted the button off my shirt which he was holding on to, and I ran away. I tried to out-run him, and that tickled him. I sure gave the ground fits with my feet. But them whippings done me good. They broke me up from thieving and made a man of me.

WILL ADAMS

My folks always belonged to the Calvins and wore their name till emancipation . . . . The Calvins always thought lots of their niggers, and Grandma Maria said, "Why shouldn't they? It was their money." She said there were plenty of Indians here when they settled this country, and they bought and traded with them without killing them, if they could. The Indians were poor folks, who just pilfered and loafed around all the time. The Negroes were a heap sight better off than they were, because we had plenty to eat and a place to stay.

Young Massa Tom was my special massa, and he still lives here. Old Dave seemed to think more of his niggers than anybody, and we

19

thought lots of our white folks. My pa was leader on the farm, and there wasn't an overseer or driver. When pa whipped a nigger, he didn't need to go to Massa Dave, but pa said, "Go away, you nigger, Freeman didn't whip you for nothing." Massa Dave always believed pa, because he told the truth.

One time a peddler came to our house, and after supper he went to see about his pony. Pa had fed that pony fifteen ears of corn. The peddler told massa his pony hadn't been fed nothing, and massa got mad and said, "Be on your way if you're going to accuse my niggers of lying."

ROSE WILLIAMS

Massa Black had a big plantation, but he had more niggers than he needed to work on that place, cause he was a nigger trader. He traded and bought and sold all the time.

I have the correct memorandum of when the war started. Massa Black sold us right then. Mammy and pappy were powerfully glad to get sold, and they and I were put on the block with about ten other niggers. When we got to the trading block, there were lots of white folks there who came to look us over. One man showed an interest in pappy. His name was Hawkins. He talked to pappy, and pappy talked to him and said, "Those are my woman and child. Please buy all of us and have mercy on us." Massa Hawkins said, "That gal is a likely-looking nigger; she is portly and strong, but three are more than I want, I guess."

The sale started and before long pappy was put on the block. Massa Hawkins won the bid for pappy, and when mammy was put on the block, he won the bid for her. Then there were three or four other niggers sold before my turn came. Then Massa Black called me to the block, and the auction man said, "What am I offered for this portly, strong young wench? She's never been abused and will make a good breeder."

I wanted to hear Massa Hawkins bid, but he said nothing. Two other men were bidding against each other, and I sure was worried. There were tears coming down my cheeks cause I was being sold to some men that would make separation from my mammy. One man bidded $500, and the auction man asked, "Do I hear more? She is going at $500." Then someone said $525.00, and the auction man said, "She is sold for $525.00 to Massa Hawkins." Was I glad and excited. I was quivering all over.

There's one thing Massa Hawkins did to me that I can't shut from my mind. I know he didn't do it for meanness, but I always held it against him. What he did was force me to live with that nigger, Rufus, against my wants.

20

After I had been at his place about a year, the massa came to me and said, "You're going to live with Rufus in that cabin over yonder. Go fix it for living." I was about sixteen years old and had no learning, And I was just an ignorant child. I thought that meant for me to tend the cabin for Rufus and some other niggers. Well, that was the start of pestigation for me.

I took charge of the cabin after work was done and fixed supper. Now, I didn't like that Rufus, cause he was a bully. He was big and cause of that he thought everybody should do what he said. We had supper, then I went here and there talking till I was ready for sleep, and then I got in the bunk. After I was in, that nigger came and crawled in the bunk with me before I knew it. I said, "What do you mean, you fool nigger." He said for me to hush the mouth. "This is my bunk, too," he said.

"You're touched in the head. Get out." I told him, and I put the feet against him and gave him a shove, and out he went on the floor before he knew what I was doing. That nigger jumped up, and he was mad. He looked like a wild boar. He started for the bunk, and I jumped quickly for the poker. It was about three feet long, and when he came at me I let him have it over the head. Did that nigger stop in his tracks? I'll say he did. He looked at me steady for a minute, and you could tell he was thinking hard. Then he went and sat on the bench and said, "Just wait. You think you is smart, but you are foolish in the head. They're going to learn you something."

"Hush your big mouth and stay away from this nigger. That's all I want," I said, and just sat and held that poker in the hand. He just sat, looking like the bull. There we sat and sat for about an hour, and then he went out, and I barred the door.

The next day I went to see the missy and told her what Rufus wanted, and missy said that was the massa's wishes. She said, "You are the portly gal, and Rufus is the portly man. The massa wants you to bring forth portly children."

I was thinking about what the missy said, but said to myself, "I'm not going to live with that Rufus." That night when he came in the cabin I grabbed the poker and sat on the bench and said, "Get away from me, nigger, before I bust your brains out and stomp on them." He said nothing and got out.

The next day the massa called me and told me, "Woman, I've paid big money for you, and I've done that for the cause I want you to raise me children. I've put you to live with Rufus for that purpose. Now, if you don't want a whipping at the stake, you do what I want."

I thought about massa buying me off of the block and saving me from being separated from my folks and about whipping at the stake.

21

There I was. What was I to do? So I decided to do as massa wished, and so I yielded.

J. W. TERRILL

My father took me away from my mother when I was six weeks old and gave me to my grandmother, who was real old at the time. Just before she died she gave me back to my father, who was my mammy's massa. He was an old bachelor and ran a saloon, and he was white, but my mammy was a nigger. He was mean to me.

Finally, my father let his sister take me and raise me with her children. She was good to me, but before he let her have me he willed that I must wear a bell till I was 21 years old, strapped around my shoulder with the bell about three feet from my head in a steel frame. That was for punishment for being born into the world the son of a white man and my mammy a nigger slave. I wore this frame with the bell where I couldn't reach the clapper day and night. I never knew what it was to lay down in bed and get a good night's sleep till I was about 17 years old, when my father died and my missy took the bell off of me.

Before my father gave me to his sister, I was tied and strapped to a tree and whipped like a beast by my father till I was unconscious and then left strapped to a tree all night in cold and rainy weather. My father was very mean. He and his sister brought me to Texas, to North Gulch, when I was about 12 years old. He brought my mammy, too, and made her come and be his mistress one night every week. He would have killed every one of his slaves rather than see us go free, especially me and my mammy.

My missy was pretty good to me, when my father wasn't right around. But he wouldn't let her give me anything to eat but cornbread and water and little sweet taters and just enough of that to keep me alive. I was always hungry. My mammy had a boy called Frank Adds and a girl called Marie Adds, which she gave birth to by her colored husband, but I never got to play with them.

I wore the bell night and day, and my father would chain me to a tree till I nearly died from the cold and being so hungry. My father didn't believe in church, and my missy believed there was a Lord, but I wouldn't have believed her if she tried to teach me about religion, cause my father told me I wasn't any more than a damn mule. I slept on a chair and tried to rest till my father died, and then I sang all day, cause I knew I wouldn't be treated so mean. When Missy took that bell off of me I thought I was in Heaven, cause I could lie down and go to sleep. When I didn't have it, I couldn't wake up for a long time, and when I did wake up I'd be scared to death I'd see my father with his whip and that old bell. I'd jump out of bed and run till I gave out, for fear he'd come back and get me.

22

BEN SIMPSON

When night time came the massa locked the chain around our necks and then locked it around a tree. Boss, our bed was the ground. All he fed us was raw meat and green corn. Boss, I ate many a green weed. I was hungry. He never let us eat at noon; he worked us all day without stopping. We went naked, that's the way he worked us. We never had any clothes.

He branded us. He branded my mother before we left Georgia. Boss, he nearly killed her. He branded her on the breast, then between the shoulders. He branded all of us.

My sister, Emma, was the only woman he had till he married. Emma was the wife of all seven Negro slaves. He sold her when she was about fifteen, just before her baby was born. I never saw her since.

Boss, Massa was an outlaw. He came to Texas and dealt in stolen horses. Just before he was hung for stealing horses, he married a young Spanish gal. He was sure mean to her, whipped her cause she wanted him to leave her alone and live right. Bless her heart, she was the best gal in the world. She was the best thing God ever put life into in the world. She cried and cried every time massa went off. She let us loose, and she fed us good one time while he was gone. Missy Selena, she turned us loose, and we washed in the creek close by. She just fastened the chain on us and gave us a great big pot of cooked meat and corn, and up he rode. He never said a word but came to see what we were eating. He picked up his whip and whipped her till she fell. If I could have gotten loose I would have killed him. I swore if I ever got loose I'd kill him. But before long after he failed to come home, some people found him hanging to a tree.

HENDERSON PERKINS

Marster Garner ran a tavern; they call them hotels now. My mammy was cook for the tavern. The other nigger was named Gib, and I had to do the work around the place and take grist to the water mill to grind. Marster had the farm, too, and had seven niggers on that place, and sometimes I went there to help.

Well, about treatment, you can't say Marster Garner was the best man who ever lived. I'll just say he was O.K. I've never heard him say one cross word to my mammy. He had his own still and gave the toddy to us lots of times. I've got a few whippings, but it was my fault. It was because of devilment. I'll tell you about some. I drove the oxen and the two-wheeled cart to go to the water mill and such. In them days, it was a great insult to say, "You have bread and rotten egg for supper." I was going to the mill one day, past the school, and I said that to the children. I thought the teacher wouldn't let them come

23

out, but I made a mistake, for it was like yellow jackets pouring out
of the hive. They threw sticks and stones at us, and that surprised the
oxen and ox and he ran. The road was rough and that cart had no
spring and the corn was scattered on the road. Marster whipped us
for that. Not hard, just a couple of licks.

HIRAM MAYES

The first thing I remember back in slavery times was getting in massa's
strawberry patch. He was right proud of that patch and got after us
plenty. There was little Tim Edgar, that's the white boy, and me. Tim,
he's still living down in Wallisville. Old massa he cut us both a couple
of times for thieving his strawberries, just gave us a brush or two
to scare us. That was the only time he ever did whip me, and you
couldn't hardly call that a whipping.

JAMES HAYES

The master took good care of us and sometimes gave us money, about
25¢, and let us go to town. That was when he was happy and celebrated.
We spent all the money on candy and sweet drinks. Master never crowded us about the work, and never gave any of us whippings. I several
times needed a whipping, but the master never gave this nigger more'n
a good scolding. The nearest I came to getting whipped was once when
I stole a plate of biscuits off of the table. I wasn't in need of them,
but the devil in me caused me to do it. Master and all the folks came
in and sat down, and he asked for the biscuits, and I was under the
house and could hear them talk. The cook said, "I've put the biscuits
on the table." Master said, "If you did, the hound got them." Cook
said, "If a hound got them, it was a two-legged one, cause the plate
is gone too." I'd made the mistake of taking the plate. Master gave
me the worst scolding I ever had and that learned me a lesson.

ROSANNA FRAZIER

All of us little children, black and white, played together and Massa
Frazier, he raised us. His children were called Sis and Texana and
Robert and John. Massa Frazier he treated us nice, and the other white
folks called us "free niggers" and wouldn't allow us on their places.
They were afraid their niggers would get dissatisfied with their own
treatment. Sure's your born, if one of us got round them plantations,
they just cut us to pieces with the whip. Some of them white folks
sure were mean, and they worked the niggers all day in the sun and
cut them with the whip, and sure done them up bad. That was on
other places, not on ours.

Massa Frazier, he didn't work us too hard and gave Saturday and

24

Sunday off. He's all right and gave good food. People sure would rare off from him, because he was too good. He was the Methodist preacher and furnished us church. Sometimes he had camp meeting, and they cooked out-doors with the skillets. Sometimes he had corn shucking time, and we had hog meat and meal bread and whiskey and eggnog and chicken.

WALTER RIMM

Those sales are one thing that made an impression on me. I heard the folks whisper about going to have the sale, and about noon there was a crowd of folks in the front yard, and a nigger trader with his slaves. They set up a platform in the middle of the yard, and one white man got on that and another white man came up and had a white woman with him. She appeared to be about fifteen years old and had long, black hair down her back. They put her on the platform, and then I heard a scream, and a woman who looked like the gal cried out, "I'll cut my throat if my daughter is sold." The white man went and talked to her and finally allowed her to take the young gal away with her. That sure stirred up a commotion amongst the white folks, but they said that gal had just a little nigger blood and could be sold for a slave, but she looked as white as anybody I ever saw.

MINTIE MARIA MILLER

They said they were going to sell me, cause Miss Nancy's father-in-law died, and they got rid of some of us. She didn't want to sell me so she told me to be sassy, and no one would buy me. They took me to Houston and to the market, and a man called George Fraser sold the slaves. The market was an open house, more like a shed. We all stood to one side till our turn came. There was nothing else you could do.

They stood me on a block of wood, and a man bid me in. I felt mad. You see I was young then, too young to know better. I didn't know what they sold me for, but the man who bought me made me open my mouth while he looked at my teeth. They did us all that way, sold us like you sell a horse. Then my old master bade me good-by and tried to give me a dog, but I remembered what Miss Nancy had said, and I sassed him and slapped the dog out of his hand. So the man who bought me said, "When one o'clock comes you've got to sell her again, she's sassy. If she did me that way I'd kill her." So they sold me twice in the same day. There were two sellings that day.

JAMES BROWN

Another thing that massa did powerful good was trade the niggers. He bought and sold them all the time. You see, there were traders that

traveled from place to place them days and they took sometimes as
many as 100 niggers to trade. There were sheds outside of town, where
they kept the niggers when they came to town.

The massa and the trader talked this way: "How you trade?" "I'll
give you even trade." "No, I want $25.00 for the difference." "I'll
give you $5.00." That's the way they talked on and on. Maybe they'd
make the trade, and maybe they didn't.

They had auctions sometimes, and massa always attended them.
At the auction, I've seen them sell a family. Maybe one man would
buy the mammy, another buy the pappy, and another buy all the
children or maybe just one, like that. I've seen them cry like they were
at a funeral when they were parted. They had to drag them away.

When the auction began, he said: "This nigger is so and so old, he's never
been abused, he's sound as a dollar. Just look at the muscle and the big
shoulders. He's worth a thousand of any man's money. How much am I
offered?" Then the bidding started. It went like this: "$200, I hear, do I
hear $250, do I hear $300." Then the nigger took his clothes—they had
one extra suit—and went with the man that bought him.

TOM HOLLAND

I saw slaves sold and auctioned off, because I was put up to the highest
bidder myself. Massa traded me to William Green just before the war,
for a hundred acres of land at $1.00 an acre. He thought I'd never be
much account, cause I had the glass eye . . . . All the hollering and
bawling took place, and when he sold me it took me most a year to
get over it, but there I was, belonging to another man.

If we went off without a pass we always went two at a time. We
slipped off when we got a chance to see young folks on some other
place. The patrollers caught me one night, and Lord have mercy on
me, they stretched me over a log and hit me thirty-nine licks with a
rawhide loaded with rock, and every time they hit me the blood and
hide flew. They drove me home to massa and told him and he called
an old mammy to doctor my back, and I couldn't work for four days.
That never kept me from slipping off again, but I was more careful
the next time.

We'd go and fall right in at the door of the quarters at night, so
massa and the patrollers thought we were real tired and let us alone
and not watch us. That very night we were planning to slip off somewhere to see a negro gal or wife, or to have a big time, especially when
the moon shone all night so we could see. It wouldn't do to have
torch lights. They were about all the kind of lights we had them days,
and if we made light, massa came to see what we were doing, and it
was just too bad for the stray nigger!

C. B. MCRAY

We had a foreman named Charlie. It was his duty to keep the place stocked with wood. He took slaves and worked the wood patches when it was needed, but once Marster came home from New Orleans and found them all suffering for want of fire. He called old Charlie and asked him why he had not gotten up plenty of wood. "Well," old Charlie said, "wood was short, and before I could get more this cold spell came, and it was too awful cold to get wood." Marster said, "You keep plenty of wood or I'm going to sell you to a mean marster." Charlie got better for a while, then he let wood get low again. So he was sold to Ballard Adams, who had the name of being hard on his slaves. Charlie couldn't do enough work to suit Marster Adams, so he put him in what's known as the "Louisiana shirt." That was a barrel with a hole cut in the bottom just big enough for Charlie to slip his head through. They pulled this on to him every morning, and then he couldn't sit down or use his arms, and could just walk around all day, the brunt of other slaves' jokes. At night they took it off and chained him to a bed. After he had worn this Louisiana shirt a month, the Marster tasked him again. He failed and ran off to the woods. So Marster Adams, he came to Marster McRay and wanted to sell Charlie back again, but he couldn't cause freedom had just come and they couldn't sell slaves any more, but Marster McRay said Charlie could come back and stay on his place if he wanted to.

MOLLY HARRELL

They used to have the little whip they used on the women. Course the field hands got it worse, but then they were men. Mr. Swanson was good and was mean. He was nice one day and mean as Hades the next. You never knew what he was going to do. But he never punished nobody except if they did something. My father was a field hand, and Mr. Swanson worked the fire out of them. Work, work— that was all they knew from the time they got up in the morning till they went to bed at night. But he wasn't hard on them like some masters were. If they were sick, they didn't have to work, and he gave them the medicine himself. If he caught them trying to play off sick, then he laid into them, or if he caught them loafing. Course I don't blame him for that, cause there ain't nothing lazier than a lazy nigger. Will was about the laziest one in the bunch. You ain't never found a lazier nigger than Will.

AUNTIE THOMAS JOHNS

One of Major Odom's niggers was whipped by a man named Steve

Owens. He got to going to see a nigger woman Owens owned, and one
night they beat him up bad. Major Odom put on his gun for Owens,
and they carried guns for each other till they died, but they never did
have a shooting.

Colonel Sims had a farm joining Major Odom's farm, and his niggers
were treated mean. He had an overseer, J. B. Mullinaz, I remember
him, and he was big and tough. He whipped a nigger man to death. He
would come out on a morning and give a long, keen yell, and say, "I'm
J. B. Mullinaz, just back from a week in Hell, where I got two new eyes,
one named Snap and Jack, and the other Take Hold. I'm going to whip
two or three niggers to death today." He lived a long time, but long
before he died his eyes turned backward in his head. I saw them that-
away. He wouldn't give his niggers much to eat and he'd make them
work all day, and just give them boiled peas with just water and no
salt and cornbread. They'd eat their lunch right out in the hot sun
and then go right back to work. Mama said she could hear them niggers
being whipped at night and yelling, "Pray, master, pray," begging
him not to beat them.

Other niggers would run away and come to Major Odom's place
and ask his niggers for something to eat. My mama would get word to
bring them food, and she'd start out to where they were hiding, and
she'd hear the hounds and the runaway niggers would have to go on
without getting nothing to eat.

MONROE BRACKINS
Our massa was tolerably good to us, to be slaves as we were. His brother
had a hired man who whipped me once with a quirt. I've heard my
father and mother tell how they whipped them. They were tied down
on a log or up to a post and whipped them till the blisters rose, then
take a paddle and open them up, and pour salt on them. Yes, man,
they whipped the women. The most I remember about that, my father
and sister were in the barn shucking corn, and the marster came in
there and whipped my sister with a cowhide whip. My father caught
a lick in the face, and he told the marster to keep his whip off of him.
So the marster started on my father, and he ran away. When he
finally came in, he was so wild his marster had to call him to get orders for work, and finally the boss shot at him, but they didn't whip
him any more. Of course, some of them whipped with more mercy.
They had a whipping post, and when they strapped them down on a
log, they called it a "strapping log."

HENRY LEWIS
They used to have old slavery-day judges and juries of white folks,

28

and they heard the case and decided how many lashes to give the darkey. They put the lash on them, but they never put no jail on them. I saw some slaves in chains and heard of one massa who had the place in the fence with the hole cut out for the nigger's neck. They hitched up the board, and the nigger put his head through the hole and then they beat him with a lash with holes bored in it, and every hole raised the blister. Then he busted them blisters with the handsaw, and they put salt and pepper in the bucket water and annointed them blisters with the mop dipped in the water. They did that when they were in particular bad humor, if a nigger hadn't chopped enough cotton or corn. Sometimes an overseer killed a nigger, and they didn't do anything to him except make him pay for the nigger.

There used to be nigger traders who came through the country with the herd of niggers, just like cattlemen with the herd of cattle. They fixed camp and the pen on the ridge outside of town and people who wanted to buy more slaves went there. They had a block and made the slaves get up on that. Maybe one said, "I'll give you $200," and when they were through, the slave was sold to the highest bidder. Old Massa warned us to look out and not let the trader catch us, cause the trader'd just as soon steal a nigger as sell him.

BILL MCRAY

We had a good master, but some of the neighbors treated their slaves rough. Old Dr. Neyland of Jasper, he had 75 or 80 slaves and he was rich and hard on the slaves. One day two ran away, Tom and Ike, and Dr. Neyland took the bloodhounds and caught those two niggers and brought them in. One of the niggers took a club and knocked one of the hounds in the head and killed him. They cooked that dog and made them niggers eat part of him. Then they gave both of them a beating.

The old log jail in Jasper, it used to stand where the Fish store is now. They had a place on the other side of the jail where they whipped niggers. The whipping post was a big log. They made the niggers lie down on it and strapped them to it. I was a little boy then, and me and two white boys, Coley McRay and Henry Munn, we used to slip around and watch them. Coley and Henry both grew up and went to war, but neither one came back.

Sam Swan, he was sheriff, and he caught two runaway niggers one day. They were brothers, and they were named Rufe and John Grant. Well, he took them and put them in jail and some of the men got them out and took them down to the whipping post and then strapped them down and gave them one terrible lashing and then threw salt in their wounds and you could hear them niggers holler for a mile. Then they took them back to the farm to work.

Bill McRay, age 86

They hanged a good many niggers around Jasper. In slavery times they hanged a nigger named Jim Henderson at Mayhew Pond. We boys were there and marked the tree. Two colored men, Tom Jefferson and Sam Powell, they killed another nigger, and they hanged them to the old white oak tree which is south of the Jasper Court House.

 CHAPTER III

THE NECESSITIES OF LIFE

MOSES HURSEY

We lived quite well considering. We had a little log house like the rest of the niggers, and I played around the place. Eating time came, and my mother brought a pot of beans or beans and cornbread or side meat. I had another brother and sister coming along then, and we had tin plates and cups and knives and spoons, and always sat to eat our food.

We had enough clothes, such as they were. I wore shirt-tales out of duckings till I was a big boy. All the little niggers wore shirt-tails. My mother had fair to middling cotton dresses.

ABRAM SELLS

You see, we all had pretty good times on Massa Rimes' plantation. None of them cared about being set free. They had to work hard all the time, but that didn't mean so much, cause they had to work if they were on their own too. The old folks were allowed Saturday evening off or when they were sick, and us little ones, we did not do much but bring in the wood and kindle the fires and tote water and help wash clothes and feed the little pigs and chickens . . . . They fed all us nigger children in a big trough made out of wood, maybe more of a wooden tray, dug out of soft timber like magnolia or cypress. They put it under a tree in the shade in summer time and gave each child a wooden spoon, then mixed all the food up in the trough, and we went to eat. Most of the food was potlicker, just common old potlicker—turnip greens and juice, Irish taters, and the juice, cabbages

32

and peas and beans, just about anything that made potlicker. All of us got around like so many little pigs, and then we dished in with our wooden spoon till it was all gone.

We had lots of meat at times. Old grand-daddy was always catching rabbits in some kind of trap, mostly made out of a hollow log. He set them around in the garden and sure caught the rabbits. And possums, we had a good possum dog, sometimes two or three, and every night you heard those dogs barking in the field down by the branch. Sure enough, they had a possum treed, and we went to get him and parboil him and put him in the oven and bake him plumb tender. Then we stacked sweet potatoes around him and poured the juice over the whole thing. Now, there is something good enough for a king.

There were lots of deer and turkey and squirrel in the wild wood and somebody was out hunting nearly every day. Of course Massa Rimes' folks couldn't eat up all this meat before it spoiled, and the niggers always got a great big part of it. Then we killed lots of hogs, and then talked about eating! Oh, those chitlings, sousemeat, and the haslets, that's the liver and the lights all boiled up together. Us little niggers filled up on such as that and went to bed and most dreamed we were little pigs.

We always had plenty to eat but didn't pay much attention to clothes. Boys and gals all dressed just alike, one long shirt or dress. They called it a shirt if a boy wore it and called it a dress if the gal wore it. There was no difference, cause they were all made out of something like duck and all white. That is, they were white when you first put them on, but after you wore them a while they got kind of pig-colored, kind of gray, but still they were all the same color. We all went barefooted in summer, little ones and big ones, but in winter we had homemade shoes. They tanned the leather at home and made the shoes at home; always some old nigger could make shoes. They were more like moccasins, with laces made out of deerskin. The soles were pegged on with wooden pegs out of maple and sharpened down with a shoe knife.

We had hats made out of pine straw, long leaf pine straw, tied together in little bunches and platted around and around till it made a kind of hat. That pine straw was great stuff in those days, and we used it in lots of ways. We covered sweet potatoes with it to keep them from getting frozen, and hogs made beds out of it and folks too. Yes, sir, we slept on it. The beds had just one leg. They bored two holes in the wall up in the corner and stuck two poles in those holes and laid planks on that like slats and piled lots of pine straw on that. Then they spread a homemade blanket or quilt on that and sometimes four or five little niggers slept in there to keep them warm . . . . That was one plantation that was run exclusively by itself. Massa Rimes had a commissary or store house, where he kept whatnot things which were made on the plantation and things the slaves couldn't make for themselves. That wasn't much, cause we made our own clothes and plows and all farm tools, and we even made our own plow line out of cotton, and if we ran short of cotton sometimes we made them out of bear grass, and we made buttons for our clothes.

ANN HAWTHORNE

Yes, I remember the house I was raised in. It was just a one-room log house. There was an old Georgia hoss bed in it. It was up pretty high, and us children had to get on a box to get in that bed. The mattress was made out of straw. Sometimes they made them in cotton sacks, and sometimes they put them in a tick that they wove on the loom. I had an aunt who was the weaver. She wove all the time for old massa. She used to weave all our clothes.

We did our playing around that big house, but that front gate, we mustn't go outside that. We used to jump the rope and play ring plays and such. You know how they yoke the hands together? That's the way we used to and go around and around singing our little jump-up songs. Then we just played around lots of times anything that happened to come in our minds.

They fed us good back in slavery, gave us plenty of meat and bread and greens and things. Yeah, they fed us good, and we had plenty of cornbread. That's the reason I'm a cornbread eater now. I ain't no flour-bread eater. I love my cornbread. We all ate out of one big pan. They gave each little nigger a big iron spoon, and we sure went to it. They gave us milk in a separate vessel, and they gave everyone a slice of meat in our greens. And they never must take the other fellow's piece of meat. Everything better go along smooth with us children. We'd better eat and shut our mouths. We mustn't raise no squall.

In good weather they fed us under a big tree out in the yard. And we'd better leave everything clean and no litter around. In the winter time they fed us in the kitchen.

Us gals wore plain, long-waisted dresses.. They were cut straight and with long waists, and they buttoned down the back.

There was a colored man who made shoes for the slaves to wear in the winter time. He made them out of rough red russet leather. That leather was hard, and lots of times it made blisters on our feet. I used to be glad when summer time came so I could go barefoot.

They had cabins for the slaves to live in. There was just one room, and one family in the cabin. Some of them were bigger than others, and they put a big family in a big cabin and a little family in a little cabin.

When any of the slaves got sick, old mistress and my gramma they doctored them. The old mistress she was a pretty good doctor. When us children got sick they got herbs, or they gave us castor oil and turpentine. If it got to be a serious ailment they sent for the regular doctor. They used to hang asafoetida around our neck in a little bag to keep us from catching the whooping cough and the measles.

Master used to sit around and watch us children play. He enjoyed that. Sometimes he had a wagon load of watermelons hauled up from the field and cut them. Every child had a side of watermelon. And we had all the sugar cane and sweet potatoes we wanted.

They had a big smokehouse. They had a big hog killing time, and they dried and salted the meat in a big, long trough. They got oak and ash and hickory wood and made a fire under it and smoked it. My gramma toted the key to that smokehouse, and old mistress she'd tell her what to go and get for the white folks and the colored folks.

STEARLIN ARNWINE

My mammy belonged to Master Albertus Arnwine, and he was never married. He owned four women, my mother, Ann; my grandmother, Gracie; and my Aunt Winnie and Aunt Mary. He didn't own any nigger men, except the children of these women. Grandma lived in the house with Massa Arnwine, and the rest of us lived in cabins in the yard.

The kitchen was out in the yard, and I had to carry the victuals to the big dining room. When dinner was over, Massa John took a nap and I had to fan him, and Lordy me, I'd get so sleepy. I can hear him now, for he'd wake up and say, "Go get me a drink out of the northeast corner of the well."

We had straw and grass beds; we put it in sacks on the ground and slept on the sacks. I don't remember how much land Massa John had, but it was a big place, and we had lots of slaves. Us children had supper early in the evening, and it was mostly cornbread and hog meat and milk. We all ate from a big pot. I learned to spin and weave and knit and made lots of socks.

Massa John had two step-daughters, Miss Mollie and Miss Laura, and they went to school at Rusk. It was my job to take them there every Monday morning on horses and go back after them Friday afternoon.

I never earned any money before freedom came, but once my brother-in-law gave me five dollars. I was so proud of it, I showed it to the ladies and one of them said, "You don't need that," and she gave me two sticks of candy and took the money. But I didn't know any better then.

BETTY POWERS

Mammy and pappy and us twelve children lived in one cabin, so mammy had to cook for fourteen people, besides her field work. She was up way before daylight fixing breakfast and fixed supper after dark with a pine knot torch to make the light. She cooked on the fireplace in winter and in the yard in the summer. All the rations were measured out Sunday morning, and it had to do for the week. It was not enough for heavy eats, and we had to be real careful or we went hungry. We had cornmeal and molasses and taters and peas and beans and milk. Those short rations caused plenty of trouble, cause niggers had to steal food, and it was a whipping if they got caught. They were in a fix if they couldn't work for being hungry, cause it was the whipping then, sure, so they had to steal and most of them did and took the whipping. They had the full stomach anyway.

The babies had plenty of food, so they grew up into strong portly men and women. They stayed in the nursery while their mammies worked in the fields and had plenty of milk with cornbread crumbled up in it, and potlicker, too, and honey and molasses on bread.

. . . Did we have weddings? . . . You know better than that. Those colored folks were just put together. The massa said, "Jim and Nancy, you go live together," and when that order was given, it better be done. They thought nothing on the plantation about the feelings of the women, and there was no respect for them. The overseer and white men took advantage of the women like they wanted to. The women had better not make a fuss about such. If she did, it was the whipping for her. I sure thank the Lord surrender came before I was old enough to stand for such. Yes, sir, surrender saved this nigger from such.

HARRIET BARTLETT

They put me to cooking when I was a little kid, and people now say that Aunt Harriet is the best cook in Madisonville. Master had a great big garden and plenty to eat. I cooked a big skillet plumb full of corn at the time, and all had plenty of meat. Master, he stopped out and killed a great big deer and put it in a great big pot and cooked it. Then we had cornbread and syrup.

We had log quarters with stick posts for beds and deerskin stretched over it. Then we pulled moss and threw over that. I had a good master, bless his soul. Missy, she was plumb good. She was sick all the time, and they never had white children. They lived in a big log house, four rooms in it and the great hall both ways through it.

SILVIA KING

Marse Jones and old miss found out about my cooking and took me into the house to cook for them. The dishes and things were awful queer to me, compared to what I had been brought up to use in France. I mostly cooked after that, but I was a powerful big woman when I was young, and when they got in a tight place, I helped out in the fields.

Before long Marse Jones decided to move. He always said he was going to get where he couldn't hear his neighbor's cowhorn, and he did. There wasn't nothing but woods and grass land, no houses, no roads, no bridges, no neighbors, nothing but woods and wild animals. But he built a mighty fine house with a stone chimney six foot square at the bottom. The sill was a foot square, and the house was made of logs, but they split out two-inch planks and put it outside the logs from the ground clean up to the eaves. There weren't any nails, but the whittled out pegs. There was a well out the back and a well on the back porch by the kitchen door. It had a wheel and a rope. There was another well by the barns and one or two around the quarters, but they were fixed with a long, pole sweep. In the kitchen was the big fireplace. Marse Jones never allowed that fire to go out from October till May, and in the fall Marse or one of his sons lit the fire with a flint rock and some powder.

The store was a long way off, and the white folks loaned seeds and things to each other. If we had a toothache the blacksmith pulled it. My husband managed the ox teams. I cooked and worked in Old Miss's garden and orchard. It was big and fine, and in fruit time all the women worked from light to dark drying and serving and the like.

Old Marse was going to feed you and see that your quarters were dry and warm or know the reason why. Most every night he went around the quarters to see if there was any sickness or trouble. Everybody worked hard but had plenty to eat. Sometimes the preacher told us how to get to heaven and see the ring lights there.

The smokehouse was full of bacon sides and cured hams and barrels of lard and molasses. When a nigger wanted to eat, he just asked and got his passel. Old Miss always depended on me to spice the ham when it cured. I learned that back in the old country in France.

There was spinning and weaving cabins, long with a chimney in each end. Us women spinned all the thread and wove cloth for everybody, the white folks, too. I was the cook, but some times I hit the spinning loom and wheel fairly good. We bleached the cloth and dyed it with barks.

There was always a big woodpile in the yard, and the big, caboose kettle for rendering hog fat and beef tallow for candles and making soap. Marse always had the niggers take some apples and make cider, and he made beer, too. Most of us had cider and beer when we wanted it, but nobody got drunk. Massa would sure cut us if we did.

37

Old Miss had the floors sanded; that's where you sprinkle fine white sand over the floor and sweep it around in all kinds of pretty figures. We made a corn shuck broom.

Marse was sure a fool about his hounds and had a mighty fine pack. The boys hunted wolves and panthers and wild game like that. There were lots of wild turkeys and droves of wild prairie chickens. There were rabbits and squirrels and we made Indian pudding, made of corn-meal. It was real tasty. I cooked goose and pork and mutton and bear meet and beef and deer meat, then made the fritters and pies and dumplings. Sure wish we had that food now.

On the cold winter nights, I sat many a time spinning with two threads, one in each hand and my feet on the wheel and the baby sleeping on my lap. The boys and old men were always whittling, and it wasn't just foolishment. They whittled traps and wooden spoons and needles to make seine nets and checkers and sleds. We all sat working and singing and smoking pipes. I like my pipe right now, and have two clay pipes and keep them under the pillow. I don't aim for them pipes to get out of my sight. I have been smoking close to a hundred years now, and it takes two cans of tobacco a week to keep me going.

There weren't many doctors in them days, but always the closet was full of sipples [home remedies] and most all the old women could get medicine out of the woods. Every spring Old Miss lined up all the children and gave them a dose of garlic and rum.

ISAAC MARTIN

Old Major Wood, he was my daddy's master, and of course he was mine, too. He was well fixed. He had about seventy or eighty working slaves, and I don't know how many little niggers . . . . They didn't allow any little nigger children up in the yard around the big house, except to clean up the yard, and those who did that, they had to be just like that yard, clean as peckerwoods.

Old massa he wasn't mean. He never whipped them just if anybody said the slave ought to be whipped. They had to see him and tell him what they did before he gave the order to the overseer to whip them and they didn't get whipped.

We used to go hunting with the dogs lots of times, and lots of times we caught rabbits. There were six dogs, and the rabbits we caught were so much victuals for us. I remember one night we went out hunting and caught four or five rabbits. We took them home and cleaned and dressed them, and put them in the pot to have a big rabbit supper. I was putting some red pepper in the pot to season them, and then I rubbed my eyes with my hand and got that pepper in my eyes, and it sure burned. You know how red pepper burns when it gets in your eyes; I never will forget that red pepper. The old folks used to show us how to fix the things we caught hunting and cook them.

Old massa sure thought more of his little nigger children. He used to ride in the quarters because he liked to see them come running. The cook, she was an old woman named Forney, and she had to see after feeding the children. She had a way of calling them up. She hollered, "Tee-tee, t-e-e," and all us little niggers, we just came running. Old massa, he rode up and said, "Forney, call up them little pickaninnies," and old Forney, she lifted up her voice and hollered, "Tee, t-e-e, t-e-e," and old massa just sat up on the horse and laughed and laughed a lot to see us come running up. He liked to count how many little niggers he did have. That was fun for us, too. I remember that just like yesterday.

My old master, he lived in a big house. Oh, it was a palace. It had eight or nine rooms. It was built out of logs, and moss and clay was stuffed twixt the logs. There were boards on the outside, and it was ceilinged nice on the inside. He lived in a mansion.

They were plenty rich. Old massa, he had an old wait-in man all dressed up nice and clean. Now if you wanted to talk to old massa you had to call for that old waiting man. He came, and you told him what you wanted, and then he went and told old massa, and then he said, "Bring him in," and then you went in and saw old massa and talked your business, but you had to be nice and hold your hat under your arm.

They were big rich people. Sometimes they had parties that lasted a week. They were having their fun in their way. They came in carriages and hacks.

My father was the hostler, and he had to keep the horses and see about feeding them. They had a separate little house for the saddles. Old massa he kept good horses.

When old massa wanted to go out, he called his little nigger servant to go tell my father who was the hostler, to saddle up the horse and bring him around. Then old massa got on him. He had three steps, and he could just go up them steps and then his foot would be right at the stirrup. My daddy held the stirrup for him to put his other foot in.

I was big enough to run after him and ask him to give me a dime. He laughed and sometimes he gave me the dime. Sometimes he pitched it to me, and I ran and grabbed it and said, "Thanks master," and he laughed and laughed.

Old mistress she had a regular cook. That was my mother's mother. Everything had to be just so, and everything nice and clean.

They didn't do regular work on Sunday. Every Sunday one of the other women had to take the place of the cook so she could get off. All of them who could would get off and go to the church for the preaching. Them whose turn didn't come one Sunday would go another till they all got around to go.

When it was time to eat, the old cook she hollered out "T-e-e, t-e-e, t-e-e-e" and all us little niggers came running. She had a big tray and each of us had a vessel and a spoon. She filled our vessel, and we went to eat, and then we went back for more. We got all we wanted. They gave us supper before the hands came in from the field, and what with playing around all day and eating all we could hold in the afternoon, it wasn't long before we little niggers were ready to go to sleep.

One thing, old massa didn't want his niggers to run about. Sometimes they wanted to go over to another plantation on Sunday. Then he gave them a pass if he was willing for them to go. They had patrollers to ride from plantation to see if there were any strange niggers there.

When they wanted to marry, the man he reported to old massa. He wanted his niggers to marry on his own plantation. He gave them a nice little supper and a big dance. They had some sort of license, but old massa took care of that. He had two sons who had farms and slaves of their own. Old massa didn't care if his slaves married on his sons' farms.

They had an old woman to look after the babies when their mammies were out in the field. They had a time set for the mammies to come in and nurse the babies. The old woman she had helpers. They had a big house and cradles for those babies where the nurse took care of them.

When anybody died, they had a funeral. All the hands knocked off work to attend the funeral. They buried the dead in a homemade coffin.

JACOB BRANCH

The white folks had a good house with a brick chimney. Our quarters were the good, snug little house with flue and oven. They didn't bother to have much furniture, because they were there only to sleep. We had a homemade bench and a "Georgia Hoss" bed with hay mattress. All our cooking and eating was done in the kitchen of the big house. We had plenty to eat, too. The smokehouse was always full of white taters and cracklings hanging on the wall. We got them most anytime we wanted, just so long as we didn't waste anything. They had a big jar of buttermilk and allowed us to drink all we wanted.

LIZZIE JONES

I always lived in the house with the white folks and ate at their table when they were through and slept on the floor. We never had a school or church in slavery time. The niggers couldn't even add. None of us knew how old we were, but massa set our ages down in a big book.

I remember playing peep-squirrel and marbles and keeping house when I was a child. Massa allowed the boys and gals to court, but they couldn't marry before they were 20 years old, and they couldn't marry off the plantation. Slaves weren't married by no Good Book or law, neither. They'd just take up with each other and go up to the Big House and ask massa to let them marry. If they were old enough, he'd say to the boy, "Take her and go home."

Mammy lived across the field at the quarters, and there were so many nigger shacks it looked like a town. The slaves slept on bunks of homemade boards nailed to the wall with poles for legs, and they cooked on the fireplace. I didn't know what a stove was till after the War. Sometime they'd bake cornbread in the ashes, and every bit of the grub they ate came from the white folks, and the clothes, too. I ran them looms many a night, weaving cloth. In summer we had lots of turnips and greens and garden stuff to eat. Massa always put up several barrels of kraut and had a smokehouse full of pork for winter. We didn't have flour or lard, but hunting was good before the war, and on Saturday the men could go hunting and fishing and catch possum and rabbits and squirrels and coons.

SUSAN MERRITT

Massa Watt lived in a big house that sat on a hill so you could see it around for miles, and we lived over in the field in little log huts all huddled together. They had homemade beds nailed to the wall and baling sack mattresses, and we called them bunks. We never had any money, but we had plenty of clothes and grub and wore the same clothes all the year round. Watt made our shoes for winter himself, and he made furniture and saddles and harness and ran a grist mill and a whiskey still there on the place. That man had everything.

When the hands came in from the field at dusk dark, they had to tote water from the spring and cook and eat and be in bed when that old bell rang at nine o'clock. About dusk they called the children and gave them a piece of corn pone about the size of my hand and a tin cup of milk and put them to bed, but the grown folks ate fat pork and greens and beans and such like and had plenty of milk. Every Sunday massa gave them some flour and butter and a chicken. Lots of niggers caught a good cowhiding for slipping around and stealing a chicken before Sunday.

41

MANDY MORROW

I was born in Burnet County on massa's farm, and I had three brothers called Lewis and Monroe and Hale, and one sister, Mollie. Most of the time massa was in town, cause he had the blacksmith shop there. From what I've learned by talking with other slaves, we were lucky slaves, cause there was no such thing as whipping on our farm. Sure, there was spanking and I was the one who got them from my mammy, cause I was the pesting child, getting into something all the time. I got in the devilment.

Massa smoked, and I decided to try it, so I got one old pipe and some home-cured tobacco and went to the barn and holed up with the hay. Mammy missed me, cause everything was quiet around. She looked for me and came over to the barn and heard the crinkling of the hay. She pulled me out of that, and there was plenty of fire put on my rear, and I saw lots of smoke. I remember that experience.

We all lived in one big family, except we had a separate dining room for the colored folks. Grandpappy was the carpenter, and because of that our quarters were fixed fine and had regular windows and hand-made chairs and a real wooden floor.

Mammy and my grandma were cooks and powerful good, and they taught me, and that's how I came to be a cook. Like everybody in those days, we raised everything and made preserves and cured the meat. The hams and bacons were smoked. There was no hickory wood around, but we used the corncobs, and they made the fine flavor in the meat. Many's the day I watched the fire in that smokehouse and kept it low, to get the smoke flavor.

ADELINE CUNNINGHAM

They fed us well sometimes, if they weren't mad at us. They had a big trough just like the trough for the pigs, and they had a big gourd, and they toted the gourd full of milk and then broke the bread in the milk. Then my mammy took the gourd and filled it and gave it to us children. How'd we eat it? We had oyster shells for spoons, and the slaves came in from the fields and their hands were all dirty, and they were hungry. They dipped their dirty hands right in the trough, and we couldn't eat any of it. The women worked in the fields until they had children, and when the children were old enough to work in the fields, then the mother went to old man Foley's house. There she was a house servant and worked at spinning and weaving the cotton. They made all the clothes for old man Foley and his family and for the slaves.

No, sir, we didn't get any holidays. Sundays we ground corn, and the men split rails and hoed with the grubbing hoe. Old man Foley

had a blacksmith shop, and a slave did the blacksmithing. The slaves
built cabins with split logs, and they made the roof tight with corn
shucks and grass.

HAGAR LEWIS

Missus Mary McFarland, my mother's mistress and mine, taught us
children with her own, taught us how to read and write. She treated
us just like we were her children. We had very strict leaders, my mother
and Missus Mary. She'd say, "Mammy Lize (my mother), you'll have
to come and whip Oscar and Hagar, they're fighting." Mammy Lize
would say, "No, I won't whip them; I'll just punish 'em." And we'd
have to stand with our backs to each other. My missus never did
much whipping.

We lived in cabins made of logs and chinked with mud mortar. We
had beds that had only one leg; they fitted in each corner of the wall.
They were strong, stout. We could jump on them, and have lots of fun.
We didn't stay in quarters much. The cabins were near a creek where
willows grew, and we'd make stick horses out of them. We called it
our horse lot. On the farm was a spring that threw water high, and
we'd go fishing in a big lake on one corner of the farm. Master owned
half a league, maybe more.

My father was a slave from another farm. My mother was the cook.
She cooked it all in the same place for white folks and us. We ate the
same, when the white folks were finished. There was a big light bread
oven in the yard of the big house and in front of the quarters under
a big tree. That one baked the pies. The cabins had a big fireplace
wider than that piano there. They'd hang meat and sausages and dry
them in the fireplace and cut holes in hams and hang them there. We
also had big hogsheads filled up with flour, and corn, and wheat.

Some poor niggers were half starved. They belonged to other
people. Missus Mary would call them in to feed them when she saw
them outside the fence picking up scraps. They'd call out at night.
"Marse John, Marse John." They were afraid to come in the daytime.
Marse John'd say, "What's the matter now?" They'd say, "I'm hungry." He'd say, "Come in and get it." He cured lots of meat, for we'd
hear them hollering at night when they beat the poor niggers for
begging or stealing, or some crime.

Marse John would saddle up old Charlie and go see. He had a big
shotgun across his lap. We'd hear that old bull whip just a popping.
They'd turn them loose when Marse John got after 'em. He prosecuted
some masters for beating their slaves. He knew they were half feeding
them. One time he let us go see where they'd drug two niggers
to death with oxen, for stealing or something. I can't say we were treated

43

Hagar Lewis, age 83

bad, cause I'd be telling a story. I've always been treated good by whites, but many of the niggers were killed. They'd say bad words to the bosses, and they'd shoot 'em. We'd ask Miss Mary why did they kill old uncle so and so, and Miss Mary would say, "I don't know. It's not right to say when you don't know." I'm glad to have slavery over.

When I was turned loose Miss Mary was training me and mister to do handwork, knitting and such. Mama wouldn't let us dance, didn't want any rough children. Miss Mary'd say, when I'd get sleepy, "Owl eyes, aren't you sleepy." I'd say, "No, ma'am, anything you want us to do?" I cried to sleep in the big house with Miss Mary and the children cause my sister did. She said she was going to turn white cause she stayed with white folks, and I wanted to turn white, too.

Miss Mary'd make our Sunday dresses. My mother put colored thread in woven material, and they were pretty. We had plenty of clothes. Miss Mary saw to that. They paid my mother for every child she had that was big enough to work, and Marse John saw that others did the same.

ELLEN POLK

The plantation was on the Guadalupe River, and when there was no meat the slaves went to the river and killed wild hogs and turkeys and caught fish. We ground the corn for cornbread and made hominy. And, oh Lord, the sugar cane, and what good molasses we used to make. The slaves had pretty good times, and the boss was awfully good to them. We drank well water. In dry times we toted the water from the river for washing.

The houses were log cabins. The men slaves built them. They went into the woods and chopped down the big trees, and then made them square. Did they have tools? Sure, they had an ax and a hatchet. They split the trees in two, and that made the sides of the house, and the round side was outside. How they made those logs tight? Just with mud. Then they put the boards over the mud so it couldn't fall out. When they made the boards, they split the end of the log and put the hatchet in the place, and it made a nice, smooth board.

They made the beds like that, too. They took four sticks and laid poles in the crotches, and then they put branches crossways. No, sir, they never had springs. For a mattress, they had hay and straw, sometimes corn shucks or cobs. They slept good, too.

LEWIS JONES

My birth was in the year 1851 on the plantation of Massa Fred Tate, which was on the Colorado River. Yes, sir, that was in the State of Texas. My mammy was owned by Massa Tate, and so was my pappy

45

and all my brothers and sisters. How many brothers and sisters? Lord, all mighty. I'll tell you because you asked, and this nigger gives facts as this. Let's see. I can't recollect the number. My pappy had 12 children by my mammy and 12 by another nigger named Mary. You keep the count. Then there was Liza, he had 10 by her; and there was Mandy, he had 8 by her; and there was Betty, he had six by her. Now, let me recollect some more. I can't bring the names to mind, but there were two or three others who had had one or two children by my pappy. That was right. Close to 50 children, cause my mammy done told me. It was thisaway, my pappy was the breeding nigger.

You see, when I met a nigger on that plantation, I's most sure it was a brother or a sister, so I didn't try to keep track of them.

Massa Tate didn't give rations to each family like lots of massas, but he had the cook house and the cooks, and all the rations cooked by them, and all us niggers sat down on the long tables. There were plenty, plenty. I sure wish I could have some good rations like that now. Man, some of that ham would go fine.

We raised all the food right there on the place. Hogs? We had three, four hundred, and massa raised the corn and fed them and cured the meat. We had cornmeal and wheat flour and all the milk and butter we wanted, cause massa had about 30 cows. And there was the good old molasses, too.

MONROE BRACKINS

We had possums and coons to eat sometimes. My father, he generally cooked the coons; he would dress them and stew them and then bake them. My mother would eat them. There were plenty of rabbits, too. Sometimes when they had taters, they cooked them with them. I remember one time they had just a little patch of blackhead sugar cane. After the freedom, my mother had a kind of garden, and she planted snap beans and watermelons pretty much every year.

The master fed us tolerably well. Everything was wild; beef was free, just had to bring one in and kill it. Once in a while, on a Sunday morning, we'd get biscuit flour bread to eat. It was a treat to us. They measured the flour out, and it had to pan out just like they measured. He gave us a little something every Christmas and something good to eat. I heard my people say coffee was high, at times, and I know we didn't get no flour, only Sunday morning. We lived on cornbread, mostly, and beef and game out of the woods. That was during the war and after the war, too.

JOHN MCCOY

Old Marse John had a big place around Houston and raised cotton and corn and hogs and cows. There was lots of wilderness then, full of varmints and wildcats and bears. Old Marse taught me obedience, not to lie or steal, and he taught me with the whip. That was all the learning we got. If he caught you with the book or paper, he whipped your hand down. He didn't whip the old folks none, just the young bucks, cause they were wild, and mean, and that was the only way they taught right from wrong.

I'll tell you just like I tell everyone—folks had a heap more sense in slave times than they have now. As long as a nigger did right, old Marse protected him. Old Marse fed his niggers good, too, and we had plenty of clothes. Course they were homemade on the spinning wheel, but they were good. The shoes were just like the penitentiary shoes, only not fixed so good. Old Marse killed a cow for meat and took the hide to the tanner, and Uncle Jim made that hide into shoes. They were hard and heavy and hurt the feet, but they wore like you had iron shoes.

Old Marse didn't work his niggers Sunday like some white folks did. That was the day we had church meeting under the trees. The spirit just came down out of the sky, and you forgot all your troubles.

Slave times were the best, cause colored folks were ignorant and didn't have any sense, and in slave times white folks showed them the right way. Now they are free, and they get uppity and sassy. Some of these young bucks ought to get their heads whipped down. That'd learn them manners.

 CHAPTER IV

WORKING ON A TEXAS PLANTATION

LIZZIE HUGHES

The land was red, and they worked those big Missouri mules and sure raised something. Massa had fifty head of cows, too, and there was plenty of wild game. When massa was gone he had an overseer, but told him not to whip. He didn't believe in rushing his niggers. We had a good time on that place, and the niggers were happy. I remember the men went out in the morning singing:

> *I went to the barn with a shining, bright moon,*
> *I went to the wood a hunting a coon.*
> *The coon spied me from a sugar maple tree,*
> *Down went my gun, and up the tree went me.*
> *Nigger and coon came tumbling down.*
> *Give the hide to massa to take off to town,*
> *That coon was full of good old fat,*
> *And massa brought me a new beaver hat.*

Part of another song went like this:

> *Massa said, your breath smells of brandy,*
> *Nigger said, no, I've licked molasses candy.*

When old massa came to the lot and heard the men singing like that, he said, "Those boys are lively this morning. I'm going to get a big day's plowing done." They did, too, because those big Missouri

48

Wes Brady, age 88

mules sure tore up that red land. Sometimes they sang.

This ain't Christmas morning, just a long summer day,
Hurry up, yellow boy, and don't run away.
Grass in the cotton, and weeds in the corn,
Get in the field, cause it'll soon be morn.

WES BRADY

Some white folks might want to put me back in slavery if I told you
how we were used in slavery time, but you asked me for the truth. The
overseer straddled his big horse at three o'clock in the morning, roust-
ing the hands off to the field. He got them all lined up, and then came
back to the house for breakfast. The rows were a mile long, and no
matter how much grass was in them, if you left one sprig on your row,
they beat you nearly to death. Lots of times they weighed cotton by
candlelight. All the hands took dinner to the field in buckets, and the
overseer gave them fifteen minutes to get dinner. He'd start cuffing
some of them over the head when it was time to stop eating and go
back to work. He'd go to the house and eat his dinner, and then he'd
come back and look in all the buckets, and if a piece of anything that
was there when he left was eaten, he'd say you were losing time and
had to be whipped. He'd drive four stakes in the ground and tie a nigger down and beat him till he was raw. Then he'd take a brick and
grind it up into powder and mix it with lard and put it all over him
and roll him in a sheet. It'd be two days or more before that nigger
could work again. I saw one nigger done that way for stealing a meat
bone from the meathouse. That nigger got fifteen hundred lashes.
The little chaps would pick up egg shells and play with them, and if
the overseer saw them he'd say they were stealing eggs and give
them a beating. I saw long lines of slaves chained together driven by
a white man on a horse down the Jefferson road.

The first work I did was dropping corn, and then I worked in the cow
pen and was a sheep herder. All us house chaps had to shell a half
bushel of corn every night to feed the sheep. Many times I have walked
through the quarters when I was a little chap crying for my mother.
We mostly only saw her on Sunday. Us children were in bed when the folks
went to the field and came back. I remember waking up at night lots of
times and seeing her make a little mush on the coals in the fireplace, but
she always made sure that overseer was asleep before she did that.

One time the stock got in the field and the overseer cursed an old
man and jumped on him and broke his neck. When he saw the old man
dead, he ran off to the woods, but massa sent some nigger after him and
asked him to come back; the old man just got overheated and died.

50

MARY KINCHEON EDWARDS

We picked about 100 pounds of cotton in one basket. I didn't mind picking cotton, because I never did have a backache. I picked two and three hundred pounds a day, and one day I picked 400. Sometimes the prize was given by massa to the slave who picked the most. The prize was a big cake or some clothes. Picking cotton was not so bad, because we were used to it and had a fine time of it. I got a dress one day and a pair of shoes another day for picking most. I was so fast I took two rows at a time.

The women brought oil cloths to the field, so they could make a shady place for the children to sleep, but those who were big enough had to pick. Sometimes they sang:

O—ho, I's going home,
And cuss the old overseer.

We had an ash hopper and used drip lye for making barrels of soap and hominy. The way we tested the lye was to drop an egg in it, and if the egg floated the lye was ready to put in the grease for making the soap. We threw greasy bones in the lye, and that made the best soap. The lye ate the bones.

SARAH ASHLEY

I used to have to pick cotton, and sometimes I picked 300 pounds and toted it a mile to the cotton house. Some picked 300 to 800 pounds of cotton and had to tote the bag a whole mile to the gin. If they didn't get the work done, they got whipped till they had blisters on them. Then if they didn't do it, the man on a horse went down the rows and whipped them with a paddle made with holes in it and burst the blisters. I never got whipped, because I always got my 300 pounds. We had to go early to do that, when the horn goes early, before daylight. We had to take the victuals in the bucket to the house.

PREELY COLEMAN

I grew big enough to hoe and then to plow. We had to be ready for the field by daylight and the conch was blown, and massa called out, "All hands ready for the field." At 11:30 he blew the conch, which was the mussel shell, you know, again, and we ate dinner, and at 12:30 we had to be back at work. But massa wouldn't allow no kind of work on Sunday.

Massa Tom made us wear shoes, because there were so many snags and stumps our feet got sore, and they were red russet shoes. I'll never forget them; they were so stiff at first we could hardly stand 'em.

51

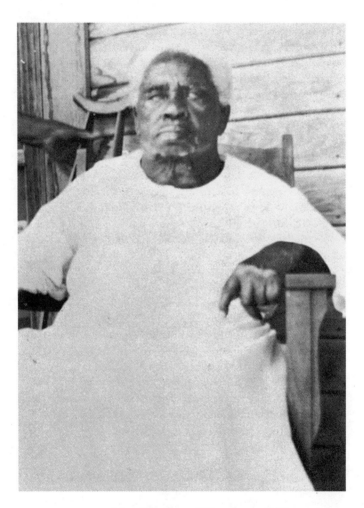

Mary Kincheon Edwards, age 127

PHOEBE HENDERSON

After they brought us to Texas in 1859, I worked in the field many
a day, plowing and hoeing, but the children didn't do much except
carry water. When they got tired, they'd say they were sick, and the
overseer let them lie down in the shade. He was a good and kindly man
and when we did wrong, and we told him he forgave us, and he didn't
whip the boys because he was afraid they'd run away.

I worked in the house, too. I spun seven curts [*sic*] a day, and
every night we ran two looms, making large curts for plow lines. We
made all our clothes. We didn't wear shoes in Georgia, but in this place
the land was rough and strong, so we couldn't go barefooted. A
black man that worked in the shop measured our feet and made us
two pairs a year.

ANDREW GOODMAN

Marse Bob didn't put his little niggers in the fields till they were old
enough to work, and the mammies were given time off from the fields
to come back to the nursing home to suck the babies. He didn't ever
put the niggers out in bad weather. He gave us something to do, in out
of the weather, like shelling corn, and the women could spin and knit.
They made us plenty of good clothes. In Summer we wore long shirts,
split up the sides, made out of lowerings—that's same as cotton sacks
were made out of. In winter we had good jeans and knitted sweaters
and knitted socks.

My pa was a shoemaker. He took a calfhide and made shoes with
the hairy sides turned in, and they were warm and kept your feet dry.
My ma spent a lot of time carding and spinning wool, and I always
had plenty of things.

SARAH FORD

The overseer was Uncle Big Jake, who was black like the rest of us,
but he was so mean I suspect the devil made him overseer down below
a long time ago. That was the bad part of Massa Charles, because he
let Uncle Jake whip the slaves so much that some like my papa who had
spirit was all the time running away. And even if your stomach is
full and you have plenty of clothes, that bullwhip on your bare hide
made you forget the good part, and that's the truth.

Uncle Big Jake sure worked the slaves from early morning till
night. When you are in the field, you'd better not lag none. When it's
falling weather the hands were put to work fixing this and that. The
women who had little children didn't have to work so hard. They
worked around the sugar house and come 11 o'clock they quit and
cared for the babies till 1 o'clock and then worked till 3 o'clock and quit.

Massa Charles ran that plantation just like a factory. Uncle Cip was sugar man, my papa tanner, and Uncle John Austin, who had a wooden leg, was shoemaker and made the shoes with brass toes.

MARTIN RUFFIN

Massa Perry had more than a thousand acres in his place and so many niggers it looked like a little town. Massa had fifteen or twenty women carding and weaving and spinning most all the time. Each nigger had his task and the children gathered berries in the woods to make dyes for clothes.

The overseer was named Charley, and there was one driver to see that everyone did his task. If he didn't they fixed him up. Those who fed the stock got up at three, and the overseer would tap a bell so many times to make them get up. The rest got up at four and worked till it was good and dark. They'd give us a hundred lashes for not doing our task. The overseer put five men on you; one on each hand, one on each foot, and one to hold your head down to the ground. You couldn't do anything but wiggle. The blood would fly before they were through with you.

The niggers sang songs in the field when they were feeling good and weren't scared of old massa. Sometimes they'd slack up on that hoe, and old massa hollered, "I'm watching you." The hands said, "Yes, sir, we see you, too." Then they brightened up on that hoe.

ADELINE MARSHALL

Captain (massa), he was a bad man, and his drivers hard, too, all the time whipping and strapping the niggers to make them work harder. It didn't make any difference to captain how little you were, you went out to the field almost as soon as you could walk. The drivers didn't use the bullwhip on the little niggers, but they played the switch on us which stung the hide plenty. Sometimes they put a nigger in the stocks and left them two or three days, didn't give them anything to eat or drink of water. If the nigger died, they just left them in a box and dug a hole out back of the horse lot and dumped them in and covered the grave up. There wasn't any preaching service or anything, put the poor nigger out of misery, that's all.

Old captain was just hard on his niggers, and I remember one day he strapped old Beans who's so old he couldn't work good any more, and in the morning they found him hanging from a tree back of the quarters. He had hung himself to escape the misery.

We worked every day except Sunday and had to do our washing then. If somebody got sick week days, he had to work Sunday to make it up. When we came in at night, we had to go right to bed. They didn't allow any light in the quarters, and you'd better be in bed if you didn't want a whipping.

WASH INGRAM

Massa Ingram had a pig plantation down near Carthage and lots of niggers. He also bought land, cleared it, and sold it. I plowed with oxen. We had an overseer and several taskmasters. They whipped the niggers for not working right, or for running away, or pilfering around massa's house. We woke up at four o'clock and worked from sunup to sundown. They gave us an hour for dinner. Those who worked around the house ate at tables with plates. Those who worked in the field were driven in from work and fed just like horses at a big, long wooden trough. They had to eat with a wooden spoon. The trough and the food were clean and there was plenty of it, and we stood up to eat. We went to bed soon after supper during the week for that's about all we felt like doing after working twelve hours.

SUSAN MERRITT

The hands were woken with the big bell, and when massa pulled the bell rope the niggers fell out of those beds like rain falling. They were in that field before daylight and stayed till dusk dark. They worked clear up till Saturday night, and then washed their clothes, and sometimes they got through in time for the party.

Massa Watt didn't have an overseer, but he had a nigger driver who was just as bad. H carried a long whip around the neck, and I've seen him tie niggers to a tree and cowhide them till the blood ran down onto the ground. Sometimes the women got slothful, and not able to do their part, but they made them do it anyway. They dug a hole, about body deep, and made the women lie face down in it, and beat them nearly to death. That nigger driver beat the children for not keeping their cotton row up with the head man. Sometimes he made niggers drag long chains while they worked in the field and some of them ran off, but they shouldn't have done it, cause they chased them with hounds and nearly killed them.

ISAAC MARTIN

I had to mind the cows and the sheep. I had a mule to ride around on. It was this way. I had to mind the cows. Old massa, he planted different fields in corn, fifty or sixty or a hundred acres. When they were harvesting the corn, when they got one field done they turned the cows in so they could eat on the stalks and nubbings which were left in that field. I had to ride around and see that the cows didn't bust over from one field which they had harvested into the other field where they were working, or which hadn't been harvested yet. I just liked that, riding that mule around the field and keeping the cows in.

Then there were five or six of us boys to keep the dogs out of the sheep. You know if the dogs got in the sheep, they were apt to kill them. They had about three or four hundred of sheep. My father had to kill a mutton every Friday for the house. They brought up the sheep, and somebody held the head across a block, and my father cut the head off with a hatchet. Sheep are the pitifulest things to kill. They just give up. And they cry, too. But a goat, he doesn't give up, no sir, he talks back to you to the last.

I remember one time they were going to give a school feast, and they were going to kill a goat. They hung that goat up to a tree by his hind legs so the blood drained good. They cut his throat, that's the way they were going to kill him. That goat seemed like he kept on talking and saying "Please, God, don't kill me," to the last, but that didn't do any good. That goat just begged to the last. Massa had two or three hundred head of cattle. My grandfather, Guilford, had a mule and horse of his own. Uncle Hank was his brother, and he had the sheep department to look after. Sometimes the niggers got a sheep over, when the master bought him. Some of the niggers had a little patch around their cabin, and they raised vegetables. Old massa he bought the vegetables sometimes.

Old massa he had twenty head of cows. They gave plenty of milk. They used to get a cedar tub full of milk. The milkers they packed it on their head to the house. Us cow-pen boys had to go drive up the calfs. Cow-pen boys? Cow-pen boys were boys that kept away the calfs when they did the milking. Course, lots of times when they were free milking, we jumped on them and rode them. Whenever they caught us doing that they sure wore us out with a beating.

SAM JONES WASHINGTON

I first ran errands, and then massa taught me to ride as soon as I could sit on the horse. Then I stayed out with the cattle most of the time, and I was tickled. I sure liked to ride and rope those cattle, and massa always fixed me up with good clothes and a good horse and a good saddle. I stayed there till long after surrender.

We had stampedes from the cattle. That was customary with those critters. That meant riding the horse to turn the cattle. We rode to the side of the leader and crowded him and forced him to turn and kept forcing him, and by and by those critters were running in a circle. That kept them from scattering. That sure was dangerous riding. If the horse threw you off, those cattle would stomp you to death. Gabriel sure blew his horn for you then.

I sure enjoyed that business, cause we had good times. We went to town and had fun. One time I came near getting in trouble, but it wasn't my fault. I was in town and massa, too, and a white man came to me, and he showed the drink. "Who you belong to, nigger?" he said. "I's massa Young's nigger," I said, polite-like. "You look like the smart nigger, and I've the notion to smack you one," he said. "You'd better not smack me any," I said. You understand, that was the way massa raised me. I don't understand why some cruel white men get in the argument just for the chance to shoot a nigger. Massa was standing near by, and he came up and said, "If you touch that nigger, I'll put the bullet through you." That man saw massa had no foolishness in his words and got going. But if massa were not there, Gabriel blew his horn for this nigger's Jubilee, right then, yes, sir.

JAMES CAPE

When I was old enough to sit on the horse, they learned me to ride, tending horses. Because I was a good horse rider, they used me all the time going after horses. I went with them to Mexico. We crossed the river lots of times. I remember once when we were driving about 200 horses northwards. There was a bad hail storm which came into the face of the herd, and that herd turned and started the other way. There were five of us riders, and we had to keep them horses from scattering. I was the leader, and do you know what happened to this nigger if my horse stumbled? Right there's where I'd still be. Master gave me a new saddle for saving the horses.

ELLEN PAYNE

I mostly minded the calves and chickens and turkeys. Massa Evans used an overseer, but he didn't allow him to cut and slash his niggers, and we didn't have a hard taskmaster. There were about thirty slaves on the farm, but I am the only one living now. I loved all my white folks, and they were sweet to us.

The hands worked from sun to sun and had a task at night. Some spun or made baskets or chair bottoms or knitted socks. Some of the young ones courted and some just rambled around most all night.

There was always plenty to eat, and one nigger didn't do anything but raise gardens. They hunted coon and possum and rabbits with dogs, and the white folks killed deer and big game like that. My daddy always had some money because he made baskets and chair bottoms and sold them, and massa Evans gave every slave a patch to work, and they could sell what it produced and keep the money.

HARRIET JONES

When Miss Ellen married Marse Johnie Watson, he had me fix her up.

She had the white satin dress and pink sash and tight waist and hook skirt, so she had to go through the doors sideways. The long curls I made hang down her shoulders and a bunch of pink roses in the hand. She looked like an angel.

All the house women learned to knit the socks and head mufflers, and many is the time I have gone to town and traded socks for groceries. I cooked, too, and helped before old marse died. For everyday cooking we had corn pone and potlicker and bacon meat and mustard and turnip greens, and good, old sorghum molasses. On Sunday we had chicken or turkey or roast pig and pies and cakes and hot, salt-raising bread.

When folks visited in them days they did it right and stayed several days or a week or two. When the quality folks came for dinner, missus showed me how to wait on table. I had to come in when she rang the bell, and hold the waiter for food just right. For breakfast we had coffee and hot waffles my mammy made.

There was an old song we used to sing about the hoecake, when we were cooking them:

> If you want to bake a hoecake, to bake it good and done,
> Slap it on a nigger's heel, and hold it to the sun.

> My mammy baked a hoecake, as big as Alabama.
> She threw it against a nigger's head and it rang just like a hammer.

> The way you bake a hoecake, the old Virginia way,
>   is to wrap it round a nigger's stomach, and hold it there all day.

When it was about time for the field hands to go to work, it was getting mighty hot down here, so they went by daylight when it was cooler. Old marse had a horn, and along about four o'clock it began to blow, and you turned over and tried taking another nap, and then it went arguing; blow, how loud that old horn did blow, but the sweet smell of the air, and the early breeze blowing through the trees, and the sun peeping over the meadow made you glad to get up in the early morning.

> It's a cool and frosty morning,
> And the niggers go to work,
> With hoes upon their shoulders,
> Without a bit of shirt.

When they heard the horn blow for dinner, it was the same race, and they sang:

I went up on the meatskins,
I came down on the pone,
I hit the corn pone fifty licks,
And made the butter mean.

ANDY J. ANDERSON

I'm going to explain how it was managed on Master Haley's plantation. It was sort of like a little town, because everything we used was made right there. There was the shoemaker, and he was the tanner and made the leather from the hides. Master had about a thousand sheep, and he got the wool, and the niggers carded and spinned, and wove it, and that made all the clothes. Then master had cattle and such to provide the milk and the butter and beef meat for eating. Then he had the turkeys and chickens and the hogs and the bees. With all that, we never were hungry.

The plantation was planted in cotton, mostly, with the corn and wheat a little, because master didn't need much of them. He never sold anything but the cotton.

JACOB BRANCH

Old Lady Liza, she had three women to spin when she got ready to make the clothes for everybody. They spinned and wove and made all our clothes. We all wore shirt tails till we were about twelve or fourteen, boys and gals, too. You couldn't tell us apart.

We children started to work as soon as we could toddle. First we gathered firewood. If it was freezing or hot we had to go to toughen us up. When we got a little bigger we tended the cattle and fed horses and hogs. By the time we were good sprouts we were picking cotton and pulling cane. We were never idle. Sometimes we got far out in the field and layed down in the corn row and napped. But, Lord, if they caught you, they sure wore you out! Sunday was the only rest day, and then the white folks allowed us to play.

Massa never whipped Uncle Charley, because he was a good nigger and worked hard. It made missy mad, and one time when massa was gone she went down in the field. Charley was hoeing corn just like massa told him, just singing and happy. Old missy she said, "Nigger, I'm sure going to whip you." He said, "What are you going to whip me for? I'm doing every bit that old massa told me." But missy thought he was getting it too good, because he had never been whipped. She climbed over the fence and started down the row with the cowhide. Uncle Charley, he hadn't even raised his voice, but he cut the last weed out of that corn and commenced to wave the hoe in the air, and he said, "Missy, I don't advise you to come any step closer." That sure made her mad, but she was afraid to do anything.

Katie Darling, age about 88

One time she had another nigger named Charlie. Massa went on a trip, and she told this Charlie if he hadn't finished grinding all the cornmeal by Monday she was going to give him a thousand lashes. He tried, but he wasn't able to make that much meal, so come Monday he ran off in the bayou. That night came the big freeze, and he was down there with water up to his knees, and when massa came home and went to get him, he was so frozen he couldn't walk. They brought him to the kitchen, and old missy cussed him out. As soon as he thawed out, he died right there on the spot.

My poor mama! Every washday old missy gave her the beating. She couldn't keep the flies from specking the clothes over night. Old missy got up in the morning before mama had time to get them specks off. She snorted and said, "Renee, I'm going to teach you how to wash." Then she beat mama with the cowhide. Looked like she would cut my mama in two. Many's the time I edged up and tried to take some of them licks off my mama.

Slavery, one to another, was pretty rough. Every plantation had to answer for itself.

KATIE DARLING
Massa had six children when war came on, and I nursed all of them. I stayed in the house with them and slept on a pallet on the floor, and soon as I was big enough to tote the milk pail they put me to milking, too. Massa had more than 100 cows, and most of the time me and Violet did all the milking. We'd better be in that cowpen by five o'clock. One morning massa caught me letting one of the calves do some milking, and he let me off without whipping that time, but that didn't mean he was always good, because those cows had more feeling for us than massa and missy.

He'd whip a man for half-doing the plowing or hoeing but if they were done right he'd find something else to whip them for. At night the men had to shuck corn, and the women carded and spun. We got two pieces of clothes for winter and two for summer, but we had no shoes. We had to work Saturday all day, and if that grass was in the field, we didn't get Sunday off, either.

CAREY DAVENPORT
My mother, she worked in the big house, and she had a pretty good house to live in. It was a plank house, too, but all the other houses were made out of hewed logs. Then my father was a carpenter, and old massa let him have lumber, and he made his own furniture out of dressed lumber, and made a box to put clothes in. We never did have more than two changes of clothes.

Campbell Davis, age 85

My father used to make them old Carey plows and was good at making the mould board out of hardwood. He made the best Carey plows in that part of the country, and he made horseshoes and nails and everything out of wood. And he used to make spinning wheels and parts of looms. He was a very valuable man, and he made wheels and the hub and put the spokes in.

CAMPBELL DAVIS

Massa didn't allow an overseer on his place. One of my uncles was the driver, and massa blew the old conk shell long before daybreak and if the darkies didn't get going, you'd hear them whips cracking.

I saw one of my sisters whipped because she didn't spin enough. They pulled her clothes down to her waist and laid her down on the stomach and lashed her with the rawhide quirt. I was in the field when they whipped my Uncle Lewis for not picking enough cotton. The driver pulled his clothes down and made him lay on the ground. He wasn't tied down, but he said he was too scared to move.

JOHN ELLIS

I've done all kinds of work which it takes to run a farm. My boss he had only fourteen slaves and what was called a small farm, compared with the big plantation. After our days' work was done we would sit up at night and pick the seed out of the cotton so they could spin it into thread. Then we went out and got different kinds of bark and boiled it to get dye for the thread before it was spun into cloth. The children just had long shirts and slips made out of this homespun, and we made our shoes out of rawhide, and Lordy! They were so hard we would have to warm them by the fire and grease them with tallow to ever wear them at all.

 CHAPTER V

RUNAWAY SLAVES IN TEXAS

CALLIE SHEPHERD

Some of the niggers didn't like the treatment which their white folks gave them, and they ran away to the woods. I'd hear the nigger dogs running, and when they caught the niggers they bit them all over and tore their clothes and got the skin, too. And the niggers, they'd holler! I saw them whip niggers, cause they told the children to look. They buckled them down on the ground and laid it on their backs. Sometimes they'd lay on with a mighty heavy hand. But I never got a whipping, cause I never went with the colored generation. I sat right in the buggy with the white children and went to hear Gospel preaching.

SARAH FORD

Lord me, there's heaps of things went on in slave times that won't go on no more, because the bright light came, and it ain't dark no more for us black folks. If a nigger ran away, and they caught him, or he came back because he was hungry, I saw Uncle Jake stretch him out on the ground and tie his hands and feet to posts so he couldn't move none. Then he got a piece of iron which he called the "slut" which is like a block of wood with little holes in it, and filled the holes up with tallow and put that iron on the fire till the grease was sizzling hot and held it over the poor nigger's back and let that hot grease drop on his hide. Then he took the bullwhip and whipped up and down, and after all that he threw the poor nigger in the stockhouse and chained him up a couple days with nothing to eat. My papa carried the grease scars on his back till he died.

Massa Charles and Uncle Jake didn't like papa, because he wasn't so black, and he had spirit, because he was part Indian. If something went wrong and Uncle Big Jake said he was going to give papa a whipping, he ran off. One time he was gone a whole year, and he sure looked like a monkey when he got back with his hair standing straight on his head and face. Papa was mighty good to mama and me, and that was the only reason he ever came back from running away, to see us. He knew he'd get a whipping, but he came anyway. They never could catch papa when he ran away, because he was part Indian. Massa Charles even got old Nigger Kelly who lived over at Sandy Point to track him with his dogs, but papa waded in water, and they couldn't track him.

They knew papa was the best tanner around that part of the country, so they didn't sell him off the place. I recollect papa saying there was one place special where he hid with some German folks, the name was Ebbling, I think. When he hid there, he tanned hides on the sly like, and they fed him, and lots of mornings when we opened the cabin door, on a shelf just above was food for mama and me and sometimes store clothes. No one had seen papa, but there it was. One time he brought us dresses, and Uncle Big Jake heard about them, and he sure was mad because he couldn't catch papa, and he said to mama that he was going to whip her unless she told him where papa was. Mama said, "Before God, Uncle Jake, I don't know, because I haven't seen him since he ran away," and just then papa came around the corner of the house. He saved mama from the whipping, but papa got the hot grease dropped on him like I told you Uncle Big Jake did, and got put in the stock-house with shackles on him and kept there three days, and while he was in there mama had the going down pains, and my sister was born.

BETTY SIMMONS

When we came to Grand Cane a nigger boy got stuck on one of us house girls, and he ran away from his massa and followed us. It was a woody country, and the boy outran his chasers. I heard the dogs after him, and he was torn and bleeding with the brush, and he ran upstairs in the gin house. The dogs sat down by the door, and the dog-man who had been hired to chase him, he drove him down and threw him in the horse hole and told the two dogs to swim in and get him. The boy was so scared he yelled and hollered, but the dogs nipped and pinched him good with claws and teeth. When they let the boy out of the water hole, he was all bit up, and when his massa learned how mean the dogman had been to the boy, he refused to pay the fee.

SARAH ASHLEY

I saw a man run away, then the white men got the dogs, and they caught them and put him in the front room, and he jumped through the big window and broke the glass all up. They sure whipped him when they caught him.

The way they whipped the niggers was to strip them off naked and whip them till they made blisters and bust the blisters. Then they took the salt and red pepper and put them in the wounds. After that they washed and greased them and put something on them to keep them from bleeding to death.

JOHN BARKER

I remember my grandma and grandpa. In them days the horned toads ran over the world, and my grandpa would gather them and lay them in the fireplace till they dried and roll them with bottles until they were like ashes and then rub it on the shoe bottoms. You see, when they wanted to run away, that stuff didn't stick all on the shoes, it stuck to the track. Then they carried some of that powder and threw it as far as they could and then jumped over it and did that again till they used all the powder. That threw the common hounds off the trail altogether. But they had the bloodhounds, hell hounds we called them, and they could pick up that trail. They ran my grandpa over 100 miles and three or four days and nights and found him under a bridge. What they put on him was enough. I saw them whip runaway niggers till the blood ran down their backs and then put salt in the places.

LAURA CORNISH

One time us children were playing out in the woods and saw two old men who looked like wild men, sure enough. They had long hair all over their faces, and their shirts were all bloody. We ran and told Papa Day, and he made us take him there, and he went in the briar patch where those men were hiding. They took him around the knees and begged him not to tell their massa where they were at because they might get killed. They said they were old Lodge and Baldy, and they had run away because their massa whipped them because they couldn't work good any more. Papa Day had tears coming in his eyes. They could hardly walk, so he sent them to the house and had Aunt Mandy, the cook, fix up something to eat quick. I never saw such eating; they were so hungry. He put them in a house and told us not to say nothing. Then he rode off on his horse and went to their massa and told him about it, and just dared him to come get them. He paid the man some money, and Lodge and Baldy stayed with Papa Day, and I guess they thought they were in heaven.

GREEN CUMBY

To see the runaway slaves in the woods scared me to death. They'd try to snatch you and hold you, so you couldn't go tell. Sometimes they caught them runaway slaves, and they'd be like wild animals and have to be tamed over again. There was a white man called Henderson who had 60 bloodhounds and rented them out to run slaves. I well recollect the hounds running through our place one night, chasing the slave who killed his wife by running the harness needle through her heart. They caught him, and the patrollers took him to Henderson and hanged him.

The patrollers they chased me plenty of times, but I was lucky, because they never caught me. I slipped off to see the gal on the next plantation, and I had no pass, and they chased me, and was I scared! You should have seen me run through that brush, because I didn't dare go out on the road or the path. It nearly tore the clothes off me, but I went on and got home and slid under the house. But I'd go to see that gal every time, patrollers or no patrollers, and I got trained so I could run almost as fast as a rabbit.

ADELINE CUNNINGHAM

One of the slaves ran away, and they caught him and put his eyes out. They caught another slave that ran away and they hanged him by the arm. Yes, sir, I saw that with my own eyes; they held the slave up by one arm, then they put an iron on his knee and an iron on his feet and dragged him down, but his feet couldn't reach the ground.

CAREY DAVENPORT

Old man Jim, he ran away lots, and sometimes they got the dogs after him. He ran away one time, and it was so cold his legs got frozen, and they had to cut his legs off. Sometimes they put chains on runaway slaves and chained them to the house. I never knew of them putting bells on the slaves on our places, but over next to us they did. They had a piece that went around their shoulders and round their necks with pieces up over their heads and hung up the bell on the piece over the head.

ANDREW GOODMAN

Old man Briscoll, who had a place next to ours, was vicious cruel. He was mean to his own blood, beating his children. His slaves were afraid all the time and hated him. Old Charlie, a good old man who belonged to him, ran away and stayed six months in the woods before Briscoll caught him. The niggers used to help feed him, but one day a nigger betrayed him, and Briscoll put the dogs on him and caught him. He

67

made to Charlie like he wasn't going to hurt him none and got him to
come peacefully. Then he took him home, and he tied him and beat
him for a terrible long time. Then he took a big, pine torch and let
burning pitch drop in spots all over him. Old Charlie was sick about
four months, and then he died.

UNCLE CINTO LEWIS

I remember once I slipped away come dark from the plantation with
some others. We were slipping along quiet like, and a patroller jumped
out from behind a bush and said, "Let's see your pass." We didn't
have any, but I had a piece of paper, and I gave it to him, and he walked
to where it was more light, and then we ran, right through old burdock
bushes with briars sticking us and everything. If he caught us, we'd sure
got a hiding.

Some of the slaves ran away to the woods, and if they didn't catch
them first, they finally got hungry and came home, and then they got
a hiding. Some niggers just came from Africa, and old marse had to
watch them close, cause they were the ones that mostly ran away to
the woods.

WALTER RIMM

My pappy wasn't afraid of nothing. There were big woods all around,
and we saw lots of runaways. One old fellow named John had been a
runaway for four years, and the patrollers tried all their tricks, but
they couldn't catch him. They wanted him bad, cause it inspired other
slaves to run away if he stayed loose. They set the trap for him. They
knew he liked good eats, so they arranged for a quilting and give chitlins
and lye hominy. John came and was inside when the patrollers rode
up to the door. Everybody got quiet, and John stood near the door, and
when they started to come in, he grabbed the shovel full of hot ashes
and threw them into the patrollers' faces. He got through and ran
off, hollering "Bird in the air."

One woman named Rhodie ran off for a long spell. The hounds
wouldn't hunt her. She stole hot light bread when they put it in
the window to cool and lived on that. She told my mammy how
to keep the hounds from following you is to take black pepper
and put it in your socks and run without your shoes. It made the
hounds sneeze.

One day I was in the woods and met the nigger runaway. He came
to the cabin, and mammy made him a bacon and egg sandwich, and
we never saw him again. Maybe he got clear to Mexico, where a lot
of slaves ran to.

GILL RUFFIN

I only knew but one nigger to run away from Marster Hargrave. He slipped off and went to Shreveport. That was Peter Going. Marster missed him and went to find him. When he found him in Shreveport, he said, "Come on, Peter, you knew what you were doing and you're going to pay for it." Marster tied him behind the buggy and trotted the horses all the way back home. Then he tied Peter to a tree and made him stay there all night with nothing to eat. Neither Peter nor none of the rest of the niggers ever tried to run off after that.

ANNA MILLER

Just about a month before freedom, my sister and nigger Horace ran off. They didn't go far, and stayed in a dugout. Every night they'd sneak in and get molasses and milk and what food they could. My sister had a baby, and she nursed it every night when she came. They ran off to keep from getting a whipping. The master was mad cause they let a mule cut himself with the plow. Sis said the bee stung the mule, and he got unruly and tangled in the plow. Master said, "They can't go far and will come back when they get hungry."

FELIX HAYWOOD

Sometimes someone would come along and try to get us to run up North and be free. We used to laugh at that. There was no reason to *run* up North. All we had to do was to *walk*, but walk south, and we'd be free as soon as we crossed the Rio Grande. In Mexico you could be free. They didn't care what color you were, black, white, yellow, or blue. Hundreds of slaves did go to Mexico and got on all right. We would hear about them and how they were going to be Mexicans. They brought up their children to speak only Mexican.

But what I want to say is, we didn't have no idea of running and escaping. We were happy.

Did you ever stop to think that thinking doesn't do any good when you do it too late? Well, that's how it was with us. If every mother's son of a black had thrown away his hoe and taken up a gun to fight for his own freedom along with the Yankees, the war'd been over before it began. But we didn't do it. We couldn't help stick to our masters. We could no more shoot them than we could fly. My father and I used to talk about it. We decided we were too soft, and freedom wasn't going to be much to our good even if we had an education.

 CHAPTER VI

GLIMMERS OF JOY

JAMES W. SMITH

Massa always wanted to help his colored folks live right, and my folks always said the best time of their lives was on the old plantation. He always arranged for parties and such. Yes, sir, he wanted them to have a good time, but no foolishness, just good, clean fun. There was dancing and singing most every Saturday night. He had a little platform built for the jig contests. Colored folks came from all around to see who could jig the best. Sometimes two niggers each put a cup of water on the head and saw who could jig the hardest without spilling any. It was lots of fun.

I must tell you about the best contest we ever had. One nigger on our place was the jiggingest fellow who ever was. Everyone around tried to get somebody to best him. He could put the glass of water on his head and make his feet go like triphammers and sound like a snaredrum. He could whirl around and such, all the movement from his hips down. Now it got noised around that a fellow had been found to beat Tom, and a contest was arranged for Saturday. There was a big crowd and money was bet, but massa bet on Tom, of course.

So they started jigging. Tom started easy and got a little faster and faster. The other fellow was doing the same. They got faster and faster, and the crowd was yelling. Gosh! There was excitement! They just kept going. Tom had found his match, but there was one thing yet he hadn't done—he hadn't made the whirl. Now he did it. Everyone held his breath, and the other fellow started to make the whirl, and he made it, but just a spoonful of water slopped out of his cup, so Tom was the winner.

LEWIS JONES

Old Tom was the preacherman and musician, and he played the fiddle and banjo. Sometimes they had a jig contest; that's when they put the glass of water on the head and saw who could jig the hardest without spilling the water. Then there was enjoyment in singing. Preacher Tom set all us niggers in the circle and sang old songs. I just can't sing for you, cause I've lost my teeth and my voice is rasping, but I'll word some, such as:

> *I'm in the new Jerusalem,*
> *In the year of Jubilee.*

LUCY LEWIS

We sure had some good dances in my young days, when I was spry. We used to cut all kinds of steps, the cotillion, and the waltz, and the shotty [schottische], and all the rest of the dances of that time. My preacher used to whip me if he heard I went to dances, but I was a right smart dancing gal. I was little and sprite, and all them young bucks wanted to dance with me.

Cinto [her husband] didn't know how to do any steps, but he did fiddle. There was an old song which came back to me, "High heels and calico stockings."

> *Fare you well, Miss Nancy Hawkins,*
> *High heel shoes and calico stockings.*

AMOS CLARK

There were two fiddlers amongst us, Jim Roseborough and Tom They'd have a big barbecue for folks from miles around and had coffee and chicken and turkey and dancing and fiddling all night. Come daybreak, they were just going good. Us niggers danced back to the quarters and called:

> *All eight balance, and all eight swing,*
> *All left allemond, and right hand grind,*
> *Meet your partner and promenade, eight,*
> *Then march till you come straight.*
>
> *First lady out to couple on the right,*
> *Swing Mr. Adam and swing Miss Eve,*
> *Swing old Adam before you leave,*
> *Don't forget your own—you you're home.*

71

Eda Rains, age 94

ANDREW (SMOKEY) COLUMBUS

The hands didn't work Saturday afternoons. That's when we'd wash
our clothes and clean up for Sunday. There were parties and dances
on Saturday night for them who wanted them. But there wasn't no
whiskey drinking and fighting at the parties. Mammy didn't go to them.
She was religious and didn't believe in dancing and such like. On
Christmas massa John always gave the slaves a big dinner, and it didn't
seem like slavery time. The niggers had a sight better then than they
do now.

WASH INGRAM

The niggers had a heap better time than now. Now we work all the
time and can't get nothing. Saturday night we would have parties and
dance and play ring plays. We had the parties in a big double log house.
They would give us whiskey and wine and cherry brandy, but there
wasn't any shooting and gambling. They didn't allow it. The men and
women didn't do like they do now. If they had such carryings on as
they do now, the white folks would have whipped them good.

NANCY JACKSON

I remember one big time we done had in slavery. Massa was gone and
then we found out he wasn't gone. He left the house intending to go
on a visit, and missy and her children were gone and us niggers gave a
big ball the night they were all gone. The leader of that ball had on
massa's boots, and he sang a song he made up:

Old massa's gone to Philiman York,
and won't be back till July 4th to come;
the fact of it, I don't know he'll be back at all;
Come on you niggers and join this ball.

The night they gave that big ball, massa had blacked his face and
slipped back in the house while they were all singing and dancing and
he sat by the fireplace all the time. Directly he spat, and the nigger
who had on his boots recognized him and tried to climb up the chimney.

EDA RAINS

Now, I must tell you all about Christmas. Our biggest time was
Christmas. Massa'd give us maybe four-bits to spend as we wanted, and
maybe we'd give a string of beads or some such notion. On Christmas
Eve we played games like "Young Gal Loves Candy," or "Hide and
Whoop." We didn't know anything about Santa Claus; never were we
taught that. But we always knew what we'd get on Christmas morning.

73

Old Massa always called us together and gave us new clothes, shoes, too. He always went to town on the eve and brought back our things in a cotton sack. That old sack would be crammed full of things, and we knew it was clothes and shoes, because Massa didn't believe in foolishness. We got one pair of shoes a year, at Christmas. Most times they were red, and I'd always paint mine black. I was one nigger who didn't like red. I'd skim grease off dishwater, mix it with soot from the chimney, and paint my shoes. In winter we wore woolen clothes and got them at Christmas, too.

MANDY HADNOT

Every Christmas before old massa died he fixed me up a tree out in the woods. They put popcorn on it to trim it, and they gave me sometimes a pretty dress or shoes and plenty of candy and maybe a big, red apple. They had a big sand pile for me to play in, but I never played with any other children.

UNCLE CINTO LEWIS

Come Christmas time old marse sometimes gave us two-bits and lots of extra eats. If it came Monday, we had the week off. But we had to watch the eats, cause niggers whose massa didn't give them no Christmas snuck over and ate it all up. Sometimes we had dances, and I'd play the fiddle for white folks and colored folks both. I'd play "Young girl, old girl," "High heel shoes," and "Calico Stockings."

YACH STRINGFELLOW

In the long winter days the men sat around the fire and whittled and made butter paddles and troughs for the pigs and such and ax handles and hoe handles and box traps and figure-four traps. They made combs to get the wool clean for spinning. We took the long strip of leather and put wire in it and bent them so they'd stay, then cut them comb-like teeth, and there you are.

Come Christmas, we slaves had a big dinner and ate all day and danced till next morning. Some of the niggers from nearby plantations got their passes and came to join us. Of course there was a drop of egg-nog around and candy for the children. The white folks had their big carriage full of visitors and there were big goings on. They came from miles around. We didn't have any money, but we didn't have any place to spend it, either.

At night we sat around the fire sometimes, and the women sewed and knitted and the men whittled and told things. They talked about charms and such.

74

ANDREW GOODMAN

Once a week the slaves could have any night they wanted for a dance or frolic. Mance McQueen was a slave belonging on the Dewberry place, who could play a fiddle, and massa gave him a pass to come play for us. Marse Bob gave us chickens or killed a fresh beef and let us make molasses candy. We could choose any night, except in the fall of the year . . . . Marse always gave us from Christmas Eve through New Year's Day off to make up for the hard work in the fall.

Christmas time everybody got a present, and Marse Bob gave a big hog to every four families. We had money to buy whiskey with. In spare time we'd make cornshuck horse collars and all kinds of baskets, and Marse bought them off us. What we couldn't use, he sold for us. We'd take post oak and split it thin with drawing knives and let it get tough in the sun, and then weave it into cotton baskets and fish baskets and little fancy baskets. The men spent their money on whiskey, cause everything else was furnished. We raised our own tobacco and hung it in the barn to season, and anybody could get it when they wanted to.

JOHN SNEED

Massa John was mighty good to us children. He always gave us a little piece of money every Sunday. When he'd get in his buggy to go to Austin to sell butter, the children piled in that buggy and all over him so you couldn't see him, and he could hardly see to drive.

On Christmas all of us went to the big house and crowded around massa. He was a little man, and some black boys would carry him around on their shoulders. All knew they were going to get the present. There was a big tree with presents for everyone, white and black. Lots of eggnog and turkey and baked hogs and all kinds of things. There were always lots of white folks company at massa's house and banquets and holidays and birthdays. We liked those times, cause work slacked and food was heavy. Every last child had his birthday celebrated with the big cake and presents and maybe the quarter in silver from old massa, bless his soul. We played kissing games and ring plays, and one song was like this:

> I'm in the well,
>   How many feet?
> Five. Who'll get you out?

If it was a man, he chose the gal, and she had to kiss him to get him out of the well. If a gal was in the well, she chose the man.

Harriet Jones, age 93

HARRIET JONES

Come Christmas Miss Ellen said, "Harriet, have the Christmas tree carried in and the holly and evergreens." Then she put the candles on the tree and hung stockings up for the white children and the black children. Next morning, everybody was up before day and there was something for us all, and for the men a keg of cider or wine on the back porch, so they all had a little Christmas spirit.

The next thing was the dinner, served in the big dining room, and that was the only time I ever had such a good dinner, except when I got married and when Miss Ellen married Mr. Johnnie. After the white folks ate, they watched the servants have their dinner.

Then they had guitars and banjos and fiddles and played old Christmas tunes. Then that night marse and missie brought the children to the quarters to see the niggers have their dance. Before the dance they had Christmas supper on the long table out in the yard in front of the cabins and had wild turkey or chicken and plenty of good things to eat. When they all got through eating, they had a little fire in front of the main cabins where dancing was going on. They moved everything out of the cabin except a few chairs. Next came the fiddler and banjoer, and when they started, the caller called "heads lead off" and the first couple got in the middle of the floor, and all the couples followed till the cabin was full. Next he called, "Sashay to the right and do-si-do." Round to the right they went, then he called, "Swing your partner," and they swung him around twice, and so it went till daylight came, and then he sang this song:

It's getting mighty late when the Guinea hen squalls,
And you'd better dance now if you're going to dance at all.
If you don't watch you, you'll sing another tune,
For the sun'll rise and catch you, if you don't go soon.
For the star's getting paler, and the old gray coon,
Is sitting in the grapevine and watching the moon.

Then the dance broke up with the Virginia reel, and it was the end of a happy Christmas Day. The old massa let them frolic all night and have the next day to get over it, because it was Christmas.

MILLIE FORWARD

Before Christmas massa went to town and brought all kinds of candy and toys and said, "Millie, you go out on the gallery and holler and tell Santy not to forget to fill your stocking tonight." I hollered loud as I could, and next morning my stocking was chock full.

WILL ADAMS

Christmas we had all we could eat and drink, and after that a big party, and you ought to see those gals swinging their partners around. The massa had two niggers wrestle, and our sports and dances were big sport for the white folks. They'd sit on the gallery and watch the niggers put it on brown.

GREEN CUMBY

The best time was when the corn shucking was at hand. Then you didn't have to bother with a pass to leave the plantation, and the patrollers didn't bother you. If the patrollers caught you without a pass any other time, you'd better wish you were dead, because you would have yourself some trouble.

But the corn shucking, that was a grand time. All the masters and their black boys from plantations from miles around would be there. When we got the corn piled as high as this house, the table was spread out under the shade. All the boys that belong to old massa would take him on the packsaddle around the house, then they would bring him to the table and sit by his side. Then all the boys that belonged to Massa Bevan from another plantation took him on the packsaddle around and around the house, always singing and dancing; then they put him at the other side of the table, and they all did the same till everybody was at the table. Then they had the feast.

CAMPBELL DAVIS

The biggest day to blacks and whites was the Fourth of July. The hands were off all day and massa gave the big dinner out under the trees. He always barbecued the sheep or beef and had cakes and pies and fancy cooking. He's one of the best bosses round that country.

And on Christmas he gave us clothes and shoes and nuts and things and another big dinner, and on Christmas night the darkies sang songs for the white folks.

SILVIA KING

The children all played together, black and white. The young ones were pretty handy trapping quail and partridges and such. They didn't shoot if they could catch it some other way, cause powder and lead were scarce. They caught the deer by making the salt lick and used a spring pole to catch pigeons and birds.

The black folks got off down in the bottom and shouted and sang and prayed. They got in the ring dances. It was just a kind of shuffle, then it got faster and faster, and they got warmed up and moaned and shouted and clapped and danced. Some got exhausted and dropped out and the ring got closer. Sometimes they sang and shouted all night, but come break of day, the nigger had to get back to his cabin. Old marse had to tell them the tasks of the day.

ABE LIVINGSTON

Us boys, white boys and me, had lots of fun when we were growing up. I remember the games we played, and we'd sing this:

Marly bright, Marly Bright,
  three score and ten;
Can you get up by candle light?
  Yes, if your legs
are long and limber and light.

Sometimes we boys, not the white ones cause they couldn't go in the woods and stay all night. We built campfires and watched for witches and haunts. I saw one but what they were I don't know. By the water-hole, one tall white haunt used to come nearly every night. I couldn't say much how it looked, cause I was too scared to get close.

Moses Hursey, age about 82

CHAPTER VII

THE WORLD OF THE SPIRITS

MOSES HURSEY

On Sundays they had meeting, sometimes at our house, sometimes
at another house. Right fine meetings, too. They'd preach and pray
and sing—shout, too. I heard them get up with a powerful force of
the spirit, clapping their hands and walking around the place. They'd
shout, "I got the glory. I got that old time religion in my head." I
saw some powerful figurations of the spirit in those days. Uncle Billy
preached, and he was right good at preaching, and naturally a good
man, anyway. We'd sing:

> Sisters, won't you help me bear my cross,
> Help me bear my cross.
> I done been wearing my cross,
> I've been through all things here.
> Cause, I want to reach over Zion's hill.
> Sisters, won't you please help bear my cross
> Up over Zion's hill?

ANDERSON EDWARDS

We didn't work in the field Sunday, but they had so much stock it
kept us busy. Missy was religious and always took us to church when
she could. When we prayed by ourselves we dared not let the white
folks know it, and we turned a wash pot down to the ground to catch
the voice. We prayed a lot to be free, and the Lord heard us. We didn't
have no song books, and the Lord gave us songs, and when we sang

them at night it was just whispering, so nobody'd hear us. One went like this:

My knee bones are aching,
My body's racking with pain,
I believe I'm a child of God,
And this ain't my home,
Cause Heaven's my aim.

ANDREW GOODMAN

Old massa built us a church, and an old man, Kenneth Lyons, who was a slave for the Lyons family nearby, used to get a pass every Sunday morning and come preach to us. He was a man of good learning and the best preacher I ever heard. He baptised in a little old mudhole down back of our place. Nearly all the boys and gals got converted when they were about twelve or fifteen years old.

RICHARD CARRUTHERS

Us niggers used to have a praying ground down in the hollow and sometimes we came out of the field between 11 and 12 at night, scorching and burning up with nothing to eat, and we wanted to ask the good Lord to have mercy. We put grease in a snuff pan or bottle and made a lamp. We took a pine torch, too, and went down in the hollow to pray. Some got so joyous they started to holler loud, and we had to stop up their mouths. I saw niggers get so full of the Lord and so happy they dropped unconscious.

I never tried to conjure, but they would take hair and brass nails and thimbles and needles and mix them up in a conjure bag. But I know one thing. There was an old gin between Wilbarger and Colorado, and it was haunted with spirits of killed niggers. We used to hear that old mill humming when dark came, and we slipped up easy, but it stopped; then when you slipped away, it started up.

JULIA FRANCIS DANIELS

All the men didn't hunt on Sunday, because Uncle Joe held meeting in front of his house. We looked out the door and saw Uncle Joe setting the benches straight and setting the table out under the trees and sweeping up the leaves, and we knew there was going to be a meeting. Those were the liveliest days that there ever was. Nighttimes, too, they'd make it between them whether it'd be at our house or Uncle Joe's. We'd ask niggers from other farms and I used to say, "I liked meetings just as good as I liked a party."

CHARLOTTE BEVERLY

We used to go to the white folks' church, and if we couldn't get in we'd stand around by the door and sing.

My white missus was a Christian, and she'd find her God anywhere. She used to shout, just sit and clap her hands and say "hallelujah." I saw her shout in church, and I thought something ailed her, and I ran down an aisle and went to fanning her.

One of the slaves was a sort-of-preacher, and sometimes massa allowed him to preach to the niggers, but he had to preach with a tub over his head, because he got too happy he talked too loud. Somebody from the big house was liable to come down and make him quit because he was making a disturbance.

WILLIAM MOORE

Some Sundays we went to church some place. We always liked to go any place. A white preacher always told us to obey our masters and work hard and sing, and when we died we'd go to heaven. Marse Tom didn't mind us singing in our cabins at night, but we'd better not let him catch us praying.

Seems like niggers just got to pray. Half their life was spent in praying. Some nigger took his turn . . . to watch and see if Marse Tom was anywhere about; then they circled themselves on the floor in the cabin and prayed. They go moaning low and gentle. "Some day, some day, some day, this yoke is going to be lifted off of our shoulders."

WILLIAM M. ADAMS

There are lots of folks and educated ones, too, who say that we believe in superstition. Well, it's because they don't understand. "Member the Lord in some of His ways can be mysterious. The Bible says so. There are some things the Lord wants all folks to know, some things just the chosen few to know, and some things no one should know. Now, just because you don't know about some of the Lord's laws, it isn't superstition if some other person understands and believes in such.

There are some born to sing, some born to preach, and some born to know the signs. There are some born under the power of the devil who have the power to put injury and misery on people, and some born under the power of the Lord to do good and overcome the evil power. Now, that produces two forces, like fire and water. The evil forces start the fire, and I have the water force to put the fire out.

How did I learn such? Well, I learned it. It came to me. When the Lord gives such power to a person, it just comes to them. It was forty years ago when I first fully realized that I had the power. However, I was always interested in the working of the signs. When I was a little pickaninny, my mammy and other folks used to talk about the signs. I heard them talk about what happens to folks because a spell was put on them. The old folks in them days knew more about the signs that the Lord uses to reveal His laws than the folks of today. It is also true of the colored folks in Africa, their native land. Some of the folks laugh at their beliefs and say it is superstition, but I know how the Lord reveals His laws.

Now let me tell you of something I've seen. What is seen can't be doubted. It happened when I was a young man and before I realized that I was one who had been chose to show the power. A mule had cut his leg so that he was bleeding to death, and they couldn't stop it. An old colored man who lived near, they turned to. He came over and passed his hand over the cut. Before long the bleeding stopped, and that's the power of the Lord working through that nigger, that's all it was.

I know about a woman that had lost her mind. The doctor said it was caused by a tumor in the head. They took an x-ray picture, but there was no tumor. They gave up, and said it was a peculiar case. That woman was taken to one with the power of the good spirit, and he said it was a peculiar case for them who don't understand. This was a case of the evil spirit. Two days after the woman had her mind back.

There's lots of those kinds of cases the ordinary person never hears about. You hear of the case the doctors can't understand, nor will they respond to treatment. That was because of the evil spell that was on the persons.

About special persons being chosen to show the power, read your Bible. It says in the book of Mark, third chapter, "and He ordained twelve, that they should be with Him, that He might send them forth to preach and to have the power to heal the sick and to cast out devils." If there is no evil in people, why does the Lord say, "cast out such?" And in the fifth chapter of James, it further says, "If any are sick, let him call the elders. Let them pray over him. The prayers of faith shall save him." There it is again. Faith, that's what counts.

When I tell that I have seen many persons given up to die, and then a man with the power comes and saves such a person, then it's not for people to say it is superstition to believe in the power.

Don't forget—the agents of the devil have the power of evil. They can put misery on every kind of people. They can make trouble with the work and with the business, with the family and with the health. So folks must be on the watch all the time. Folks have business trouble because the evil power has control of them. They have the evil power cast out and save the business. There was a man in Waco who came to see me about that. He said to me everything he tried to do in the last six months turned out wrong. It started with him losing his pocket-book with $50.00 in it. He bought a carload of hay, and it caught fire, and he lost all of it. He spent $200.00 advertising a three-day sale, and it began to rain, so he lost the money. It sure was the evil power.

"Well," he said, "That's the way it goes, so I came to you."

I said to him, "It's the evil power that has you under control, and we shall cause it to be cast out." It was done, and he had no more trouble.

You want to know if persons with the power for good can be successful in casting out devils in all cases? Well, I'll answer that yes and no. They can in every case if the affected person has the faith. If the party does not have enough faith, then it will be a failure.

Wearing the coin for protection against the evil power? That is simple. Lots of folks wear such, and they use mixtures that are sprinkled in the house and such. That is a question of faith. If they have the true faith in such, it works. Otherwise, it won't.

Some folks won't think for a minute of going without lodestone or the salt and pepper mixture in the little sack, tied around their neck. Some wear the silver coin tied around their neck. All such are to keep away the effect of the evil power. When one has the faith in such and they accidently lose the charm, they sure are miserable.

An old darkey that has faith in the lodestone for the charm told me the experience he had in Atlanta once. He was carrying the hod, and the first thing he did was drop some rock on his foot. The next thing, his foot slipped as he started up the ladder, and he and the bricks dropped to the ground. It was lucky for him it wasn't far. Just a sprained ankle, and the boss sent him home for the day. He was excited and got on the street car, and when the conductor called for the fare, Rufus reached for his money, but he had lost it or forgot it at home. The conductor said he would let him pay the next time and asked where he lived. Rufus told him, and he said, "Why, nigger, you are on the wrong car." That caused Rufus to walk further with the lame foot than if he started walking in the first place. He thought there must be something wrong with the charm, and he looked for it, and it was gone! Sure enough, it was lost. He thought "Here I'll sit all day, and I won't make another move till I get the lodestone. When the children come from school, I'll send them to the drugstore for some of the stone and get fixed."

Now, now, I've been waiting for that one about the black cat crossing the road, and sure enough, it came. Let me ask you one. How many people can you find that like to have the black cat cross in front of them? That's right, no one likes that. Let this old colored person

85

Patsy Moses, age 74

inform you that it is sure the bad luck sign. It is the sign of bad luck ahead, so turn back. Stop what you're doing.

I'm telling you of two of many cases of failure to take warning from the black cat. I know a man called Miller. His wife and he were taking an auto ride and the black cat crossed the road, and he cussed a little, and he went on. Then it was not long till he turned the corner and his wife fell out of the car during the turn. When he came back and picked her up, she was dead.

Another fellow called Brown was riding horseback, and a black cat crossed the path, but he drove on. Well, it was not long till his horse stumbled and threw him. The fall broke his leg, so take a warning—don't overlook the black cat. That's a warning.

ABRAM SELLS

We children hung around close to the big house, and we had an old man that went around with us and looked after us, white children and black children, and that old man was my great grand-daddy. We sure had to mind him, cause if we didn't, we sure had bad luck. He always had the pocket full of things to conjure with. That rabbit foot, he took it out, and he worked that on you till you took the creeps and got shaking all over. There was a pocket full of fish scales, and he kind of squeaked and rattled them in his hand, and right then you wished you were dead and promised to do anything. Another thing he always had in the pocket was a little old dried-up turtle, just a mud turtle about the size of a man's thumb, the whole thing just dried up and died. With that thing he said he could do most anything, but he never used it if he didn't have to. A few times I saw him get all tangled up and bothered, and he went off by himself and sat down in a quiet place, took out this very turtle, and put it in the palm of the hand and turned it around and around and said something all the time. After awhile he got everything untwisted, and he came back with a smile on his face and maybe whistling.

My granddaddy, he could stop blood, and he could conjure off the fever and rub his fingers over warts, and they'd get away. He made oil out of rattlesnake for the rheumatism. For the cramp he got a kind of bark off of a tree, and it did the job, too. Some niggers wore brass rings to keep off the rheumatism and punched a hole in a penny or dime and wore that on the ankle to keep off sickness.

PATSY MOSES

My old grand-daddy told me all about conjures and voodoo and luck charms and signs. To dream of clear water lets you know you are on the side of God. The old voodoo doctors were those who had the most power; it seems, over the nigger before and after the war. They had meeting places in secret and a voodoo kettle, and nobody knew what was put in it, maybe snakes and spider and human blood, no telling what. Folks all came in the dark of the moon; old doctor wore his arms, and the folks crowded up close. Those who were in the voodoo meeting stripped to the waist and commenced to dance while the drum beated. They danced faster and faster and chanted and prayed till they fell down in a heap.

The armor bearers held the candles high, and when they swayed they were seized with power which sent them leaping and whirling. Then came the time that old doctor worked his spell on those he wanted to conjure. Many were the spells he casted in those days. If he couldn't work it one way, he worked it another, and when he died, did he stay buried? No, sir! He walked the street and many saw his ghost waving his arms.

The conjure doctor, old Dr. Jones, walked about in the black coat like the preacher, and wore sideburns and used roots and such for his medicine. He learned about them in the piney woods from his old granny. He didn't cast spells like the voodoo doctor, but used roots for smallpox, and rind of bacon for mumps, and sheep-wool tea for whooping cough, and for snakebite he used alum and saltpeter and bluestone mixed with brandy or whiskey.

He could break conjure spells with broth. He took his kettle and put in splinters of pine or hickory, just so they had bark on them, covered them with water, and put it in the conjure salt.

A good charm bag was made of red flannel with frog bones and a piece of snakeskin and some horse hairs and a spoonful of ashes. That bag would protect you from your enemy. If that bag was left by the doorstep, it made all kinds of misfortune and sickness and blindness and fits.

The big, black nigger in the cornfield most always had three charms around his neck to make him fortunate in love, to keep him well, and one for Lady Luck at dice to be with him. Then if you have indigestion, wear a penny around the neck.

The power of the rabbit foot is great. One nigger used it to run away with. His old granny told him to try it, and he did. He conjured himself by taking a good, soapy bath so the dogs couldn't smell him, and then they said a hoodoo over his rabbit foot, and went to the creek and got a start by wading. They didn't miss him till he was clear gone, and that showed what the rabbit foot did for him.

88

Oh, Molly Cottontail,
Be sure not to fail.
Give me your right hind foot,
My luck won't be for sale.

The graveyard rabbit was the best, killed by a cross-eyed possum. The niggers all believed General Lee carried a rabbit foot. To keep the rabbit foot's luck working, pour some whiskey on it once in a while.

If you had a horseshoe over your door, be sure it came from the left, hind foot of a white horse, but a gray horse was better than none.

Conjures are sought with the dark or light of the moon, to make things waste or grow. If a hen crows, it's best to wring her neck and bake her with cranberry sauce and gravy and forget about her crowing. Everybody knows that.

I learned all those spells from my daddy and mammy and the old folks, and most of those things work if you try them.

SILVIA KING

Old Black Tom had a little bottle and had spell roots and water in it and sulphur. He sure could find out if a nigger was going to get whipped. He had a string tied around it and said, "By sum Peter, by sum Paul, by the God that made us all, jack don't you tell me no lie, is Marse going to whip Mary, tell me?" Sure's you're born, if that jack turned to the left, the nigger got the whipping, but if Marse hadn't made up his mind to whip, that jack stood and quivered.

You white folks just go through the woods and don't know nothing. If you dig out splinters from the north side of an old pine tree that has been struck by lightning, and get them hot in an iron skillet, and burn them to ashes, then you put them in a brown paper sack. If the officers get you and you are going to have it before the judge, you get the sack and go outdoors at midnight and hold the bag of ashes in your hand and look up at the moon, but you don't open your mouth. Next morning get up early and go to the courthouse and sprinkle them ashes in the doorway, and that law trouble, it's going to get torn up just like the lightning tore up that tree.

The shoostring root is powerfully strong. If you chew on it and spit a ring around the person whom you want something from, you're going to get it. You can get more money or a job or most anything that way. I had a black cat bone, too, but it got away from me.

ROSANNA FRAZIER

Some try to tell me snow or sweat or smoke is the reason for my blindness. That ain't the reason. There's an old, old, slewfooted something from Louisiana, and they say he was the conjure man, one of them old hoodoo niggers. He got mad at me the last plum ripening time, and he made up powdered rattlesnake dust and passed that through my hair, and I sure ain't seen no more.

That's not the only thing them old conjure men do. They powder up the rattles off of the snake and tie it up in the little old rag bag, and they do devilment with it. They get old scorpions and make bad medicine. They get dirt out of the graveyard, and that dirt, after they speak on it, would make you go crazy.

When they want to conjure you, they sneak around and get the hair combing or the finger or toenail, or anything natural about your body and work the hoodoo on it.

They make the straw man or the clay man, and they put the pin in his leg and your leg is going to get hurt or sore just where they put the pin. If they put the pin through the heart, you're going to die, and there ain't nothing that can save you.

They made the charm to wear around the neck or the ankle, and they make the love powder, too, out of love vine, which grows in the woods. They boil the leaves and powder 'em. They sure work; I've done tried them.

WILLIS EASTER

I know about ghosts. First, I'll tell you a funny story. An old man named Joseph, he was pretty old and emotional. Every evening he squatted down under an oak tree. Marse Smith, he slipped up and heard Josh praying. "Oh, God, please take poor old Josh home with you." Next day, Marse Smith wrapped himself in a sheet and got in the oak tree. Old Josh came along and prayed, "Oh, God, please come take poor old Josh home with you." Marse said from the top of the tree, "Poor Josh, I've come to take you home with me." Old Josh, he rose up and saw that white shape in the tree, and he yelled, "Oh, Lord, not right now, I haven't been forgiven for all my sins." Old Josh, he was just shaking, and he busted out of there faster than a wink. That broke up his praying under that tree.

I never studied conjuring, but I know that scorpions and things they conjure with are powerful medicine. They used hair and finger-nails and tacks and dry insects and worms and bat wings and such. Mammy always tied a leather string around the babies' necks when they were teething to make them have an easy time. She used a dry frog or piece of nutmeg, too.

Mammy always told me to keep from being conjured, I should sing:

90

Keep away from me, hoodoo and witch,
Lead my path from the poorhouse gate;
I pines for golden harps and such,
Lord, I'll just sit down and wait.
Old Satan is a liar and conjurer, too,
If you don't watch out, he'll conjure you.

Them conjuremen sure are bad. They make you have pneumonia and bad luck. I carry me a jack all the time. It is the charm wrapped in red flannel. Don't know what is in it. A bossman, he fixed it for me.

I sure can find water for the well. I got a little tree limb which is like a "V." I drive the nail in the end of each branch and in the crotch. I take hold of each branch, and if I walk over water in the ground, that limb is going to turn over in my hand till it points to the ground. If money is buried, you can find it the same way.

If you fill a shoe with salt and burn it, that'll call luck to you. I wear a dime on a string around the neck and one around the ankle. That's to keep any conjuremen from setting the trick on me. That dime'll be bright if my friends are true. It is sure going to get dark if they do me wrong.

To make a jack that is sure good, get snakeroot and sassafras and a little lodestone and brimstone and asafoetida and resin and bluestone and gum arabic and a pod or two red pepper. Put this in the red flannel bag, at midnight, on the dark of the moon, and it sure'll do the work.

I knew a ghost house. I sure did. Everybody knew it, a red brick house in Waco, on Thirteenth and Washington Street. They called it the Bell house. It sure was a fine, big house, but folks couldn't use it. The white folks who owned it, they got one nigger and another to stay there. I went. Every Friday night there was a rustling sound, like the murmur of treetops, all through the house. The shutters rattled—only there weren't no shutters on them windows. Just as plain as anything, I heard a rocking, rocking. Footsteps, soft as the breath—you could hear them plain. But I stayed and hunted and couldn't find nobody nor nothing, none of them.

Then came the Friday night on the last quarter of the moon. Long about midnight something lifted me out of the cot. I heard a little child sobbing, and that rocker started, and the shutters they rattled softlike, and that rustling, mourning sound spread all through that house. I took the lantern and out in the hall I went. Right by the stairs I saw a woman, big as life, but she was thin and I saw right through her. She just walked on down that hall and paid me no mind. She made a sound like the beating of wings. I just froze. I couldn't move.

That woman just melted out the window at the end of the hall, and I left that place!

91

FLORENCE RUFFINS

Do I believe in ghosties? I sure do, and I'll tell you why I knew there are ghosties. First, I've heard and seen them, and lots of other folks I've talked to have. Then my pappy and mammy both could see them, and they had special powers, but they were good powers. They had no use for the devil spells and all such.

In the old days before surrender the colored folks talked about ghosties and haunts, but since education is for the colored folks, some of them like to say spirit instead of ghost. Now they have the church, and they say the preacher can bring the ghost—but they call it the spirit—to the meeting and talk with them. That is the spiritualist church.

I'm telling you the things I heard my pappy and mammy tell, and what I've seen for myself. What I saw, I can be the witness for, and what my mammy and pappy saw, I can be the witness for that cause I'm not going to lie about what dead people said.

There is only one way to best the ghost, and it is to call the Lord, and he will banish them. Some folks don't know how to best them, so they got tantalized bad. There was a man called Everson, and he had been a slave. The ghost came and told him to go dig in the graveyard for the pot of gold, and to go by himself. But he was afraid of the graveyard and didn't go. So the ghost appeared again, but that man didn't go till the ghost came the third time. So he went, but he took two other men with him.

Everson dug about five feet, where the ghost told him to, and his spade hit the iron box. He pried the cover off, and that box was full of gold coins, fives and tens, and twenties, in gold money—a whole bushel in that box. He hollered to the two men, and they came running, but by the time they got there, the box was sunk, and all they could see was the hole where it went down. They dug and dug, but it was no use. If he hadn't taken the men with him, he'd be rich, but the ghost didn't want those other men there.

In that there same country, there was a farm that sure was haunted Many families tried to live in that house, but were forced to move. It was supposed the niggers which the cruel master of that farm killed in slave times came back to tantalize. The ghosts came in the night and walked back and forth across the yard, and they could see them as plain as day. There was nobody who would stay on that farm.

My pappy was coming home on the horse one night, and he felt like someone was on that horse behind him. He turned and could see something. He said, "Why you get on my horse?" but there was no answer. He tried to touch that thing, but he passed his hand right through it, and he knew it was a ghost, so pappy hopped off

92

that horse and was on the ground running quicker than greased lightning. Pappy saw that horse, with the haunt on him, going through the woods like the deer.

Right here in this house, a person died and their spirits tantalize at night. It comes after we go to bed and patters on the floor with the bare feet and rattles the paper. That sure gets me all quivering. I have to get the Bible and call the Lord to banish them. But I've seen that shadow of that ghost often, and it is a man ghost, and it looks sad.

BILL THOMAS

Yes, I saw a ghost once. One night after I was living down here, I was going to Sabinal, me and another man, and a great thing passed right in front of us. It was the blackest thing you ever saw. It was about six feet long. Yes, ma'am, it sure was a ghost or something; it disappeared, and me looking at it. The other fellow that was with me, he saw it, too.

Yes, there were lots of panthers and bears there. If this ghost was a bear, it sure was a big one. We had a ghost down here on the creek which we called the "Ball Water Hole Ghost." He was seen lots of times He used to stay down there, but he hasn't been seen lately. My wife, she saw him.

ELLEN THOMAS

Yes, ma'am, I saw him walking on the train ahead of us. He had on a black hat, like a tall stovepipe hat, and a long black coat, and when we got up close he just disappeared. He was a big man, and tall, too. I didn't know which way he went; he just seemed to disappear. My oldest daughter saw him, too. Lots of folks did. He was always seen down at that water hole somewhere.

Another time, I was staying with Mrs. Reedes, Mr. Reedes was killed, and all night long he'd come back and grind coffee and sprinkle it all over us. I was so badly scared I nearly died. Next morning, there'd be coffee all over the floor. We supposed it was Mr. Reedes' ghost. They say if a person was wicked they come back like that. Once he pulled Mrs. Reedes out of bed and pitched her on the floor, and he would take dishes out of the shelves and throw them down. I couldn't stand it but a night or two and I said I was going home. Yes, ma'am, it sure was a ghost. He sure did tear up that house every night. Why, there'd be a light shine in that room just as plain as daylight, nearly. They said ghosts will run you, but I never had any run me.

SUSAN ROSS

I never did see but one ghost, but I sure saw one. I cooked at the hotel in town and had to get up and go down the railroad track to my work before it got light. One morning a great, tall something, tall and slender as a porch post, came walking along. He stepped to one side, but he didn't have any feet. I reckon he had a head, but I couldn't see it. As I passed him, I didn't say anything, and he didn't either. He didn't have time to, before I broke and ran for my life. That's the only ghost I ever saw, but I often feel the spirits close by me.

ISAAC MARTIN

I never paid any attention to talk about ghosts. I never believed in them. But one time coming from church my uncle's wife said, "Ike, did you ever see a ghost? Want to see one?" And I told her I didn't give a cent, yet I wanted to see one. She said, "I'll show you a man dressed all in white who hasn't got a head, and you're going to feel a warm breeze." After a while down the hill by the graveyard, she said, "There he goes." I looked, but I never saw anything, but I felt the warm breeze.

I used to go to see a gal, and I used to have to pass right by an old graveyard. It was all walled up with bricks, but one place they had steps over the wall so when they had to bury a body, two men could walk up those steps side by side, and that's the way they took the corpse over. Well, when I got to those steps, I heard something. Then I stopped, and I didn't hear anything. When I started walking again, I heard the noise again. I looked around, and then I saw something white come up right there where the steps went over the wall. I had a stick in my hand and next time it came up I made a rush at it and hit it. It was just a great big, old billy goat which got inside the wall and was trying to get out. He got up just when I hit him, and he lit for the woods. That's the only ghost I ever saw, and I'm glad that wasn't a ghost.

ANDERSON EDWARDS

I believe in that haunt business yet. I saw one when I was a boy, right after mammy died. I woke up and saw it come in the door, and it had a body and legs and tail and a face like a man, and it walked to the fireplace and lifted the lid off a skillet of taters which were set there and came to my bed and raised up the cover and crawled in, and I hollered so loud it woke up everybody. I told them I saw a ghost, and they said I's crazy, but I guess I knew a haunt when I saw one.

ISABELLA BOYD

That reminds me of the ghost story they used to tell about the ghost who lived in the big bridge down in the hollow. The niggers said that ghost made too much noise, with all his hollering and his rattling them chains. So that night one of us niggers who they called Charlie, he said

94

he wasn't afraid, and he was going to get him a ghost, sure enough. We didn't believe him, but pretty soon we heard a right smart wrestling with the chains and hollering down by the bridge, and after a while he came and said he got the best of that ghost, because he hadn't got strength like the man.

JOHN BARKER

Ghosties? I was taking care of a white man when he died, and I saw something about three feet high and black. I reckon I must have fainted because they had the doctor for me. And on dark nights I saw ghosties which had no head. They looked like they were wild, and they were all in different performance [positions?]. When I was going down the road and felt a hot steam and looked over my shoulder, I could see them as plain as you standing there. I saw them when my wife was with me, but she can't see them, cause some people aren't gifted to see them.

 CHAPTER VIII

THE FREEDOM WAR

WILLIAM M. ADAMS

Just before the war a white preacher came to us slaves and said: "Do you want to keep your homes where you get all to eat, and raise your children, or do you want to be free to roam around without a home, like the wild animals? If you want to keep your homes, you'd better pray for the South to win. All that want to pray for the South to win, raise the hand." We all raised our hands because we were scared not to, but we sure didn't want the South to win.

That night all the slaves had a meeting down in the hollow. Old Uncle Mack, he got up and said. "One time over in Virginia there were two old niggers, Uncle Bob and Uncle Tom. They were mad at one another, and one day they decided to have a dinner and bury the hatchet. So they sat down, and when Uncle Bob wasn't looking, Uncle Tom put some poison in Uncle Bob's food, but he saw it, and when Uncle Tom wasn't looking, Uncle Bob turned the tray around on Uncle Tom, and he got the poison food." Uncle Mack, he said, "That what we slaves are going to do, just turn the tray around and pray for the North to win."

ISABELLA BOYD

Massa Wood always took the paper, and one night they sat up a long time and did their reading. Next morning the old cook woman, she said, "Well, they have the big war, and lots of them are wounded." Before long we had to take care of some of them wounded soldiers, and they had a camp place near us. They all camped around here, and I don't know which were the Yankees and which were the Confederates.

96

Andrew Goodman, age 97

ANDY J. ANDERSON

The war broke out, and that made the big change on the master's place. He joined the army and hired a man named Delbridge for overseer. After that, the hell started to pop, because the first thing Delbridge did was cut the rations. He weighed out the meat, three pounds for the week, and he measured a peck of meal. And that wasn't enough. He half starved us niggers, and he wanted more work, and he started the whipping. I guess he started to educate them. I guess that Delbridge went to hell when he died, but I don't see how the devil could stand him.

We were not used to such, and some ran off. When they were caught, there was a whipping at the stake. But that Delbridge, he sold me to Massa House in Blanco County. I was sure glad when I was sold, but it was short of gladness, because here was another man that hell was too good for. He gave me the whipping, and the scars are still on my arms and my back, too. I'll carry them to my grave. He sent me for firewood, and when I got it loaded, the wheel hit a stump, and the team jerked, and that broke the whippletree. So he tied me to the stake, and every half hour for four hours, they laid ten lashes on my back. For the first couple hours the pain was awful. I've never forgot it. Then I'd stood so much pain that I did not feel so much, and when they took me loose, I was just about half dead. I laid in the bunk for two days, getting over that whipping, getting over it in the body but not the heart. No, sir, I have that in the heart till this day.

After that whipping I didn't have the heart to work for the massa. If I saw the cattle in the cornfield, I turned them back, instead of chasing them out. I guess that's the reason the massa sold me to his brother, Massa John. And he was good like my first massa; he never whipped me.

ANDREW GOODMAN

Marse Bob knew me better than most of the slaves, because I was around the house more. One day he called all the slaves to the yard. He only had sixty-six then, because he had divided with his son and daughter when they married. He made a little speech. He said, "I'm going to a war but I don't think I'll be gone long, and I'm turning the overseer off and leaving Andrew in charge of the place, and I want everything to go on just like I was here. Now, you all mind what Andrew says, because if you don't I'll make it rough on you when I come back home." He was joking, though, because he wouldn't have done nothing to them.

Then he said to me, "Andrew, you are old enough to be a man and look after things. Take care of Missus, and see that none of the niggers want, and try to keep the place going."

We didn't know what the war was about, but massa was gone four years. When old missus heard from him, she'd call all the slaves and tell us the news and read us his letters. Little parts of it, she wouldn't read. We never heard of him getting hurt none, but if he had, old missus wouldn't tell us cause the niggers used to cry and pray over him all the time. We never heard tell what the war was about.

JAMES HAYES

About that time the war started. The massa and his boy, Massa Ben, joined the army. The massa was a sergeant. The women folks were proud of their men folks, but they were powerfully grieved. All this time the men were away, I could tell Missy Elline and her mama were worried. They always sent me for the mail, and when I fetched it, they ran to meet me, anxious like, to open the letter, and were scared to do it. One day I fetched a letter, and I could feel it in my bones, there was trouble in that letter. Sure enough, there was trouble, heaps of it. It told that Massa Ben was killed, and that they were shipping him home. All the folks, colored and white, were crying. Missy Elline, she fainted. When the body came home, there was a powerful big funeral and after that, there was powerful weeping and sadness on that place. The women folks didn't talk much and there was no laughing like before.

During the war, things were about the same, like always, except some victuals were scarce. But we had plenty to eat, and we slaves didn't know what the war was about. I guess we were too ignorant. The white folks didn't talk about it before us. When it was over, the massa came home, and they held a big celebration. I was working in the kitchen, and they told me to cook heaps of ham, chicken, pies, cakes, sweet potatoes, and lots of vegetables. Lots of white folks came, and they ate and drank wine, then sang and danced. We colored folks joined in and were singing out in the back, "Massa's in the cold hard ground." Massa asked us to come in and sing that for the white folks, so we went in the house and sang that for the white folks, and they joined in the chorus.

NANCY KING

I saw the soldiers coming and going to the war and remember when Massa Williams left to go fight for the South. His boy, Willie, was sixteen and tended the place while massa was away. Massa done said he'd let the niggers go without fighting. He didn't think war was right, but he had to go. He deserted and came home before the war got going good, and the soldiers came for him. He ran off to the bottoms, but they were on horses and overtook him. One of them said, "Jackson, we aren't going to take you with us now, but we'll fix you so you can't run off till we get back." They put red pepper in his eyes and left. Missie cried. They came back for him in a day or two and made my father saddle up Hawk-Eye, massa's best horse. Then they rode away. One day my brother, Alex, hollered out, "Oh, Missie, yonder is the horse, at the gate, and there isn't anybody riding him. Missie threw up her hands and said, "Oh, Lord, my husband is dead." She knew somehow when he left he wasn't coming back.

HENDERSON PERKINS

When the war started Marster's girl got married to Charles Taylor, and they had a big wedding. Before the war was over, we had a hard time. The soldiers came and took all the corn, all the meat, every chicken, and all the tobacco. You couldn't buy tobacco for a dollar a pound. But we made it. We took the leaves and cured them, then placed them on the board and put hones between them. We placed a log on top and left it about a month.

After the army took the food, it was scarce for a while. Short time after the army came, the pigeons went north. If you've never seen that, it is hard to believe. They were so thick and so many, they cut off the sun like the cloud. We got lots of them and that helped with the food. I sure was glad the army didn't come any more, once was enough. I've seen squirrels traveling on the ground so thick it looked like the carpet. They were all running away from the army.

JACOB BRANCH

One morning Alex and me got up at the crack of dawn to milk. All at once came a shock that shook the earth. The big fish jumped clean out of the bay, and turtles and alligators ran out of their banks. They plumb ruined Galveston! We ran into the house, and all the dishes and things jumped out of the shelf. That was the first bombardment of Galveston. The soldiers put powder under people's houses and blew up Galveston.

Young massa Shake Stevenson, he volunteered and got killed somewhere in Virginia. Young massa Tucker Stevenson, he didn't believe in war, and he said he was never going to fight. He hid in the woods so the conscript men couldn't find him. Old man LaCour came around and said he had orders to find Tucker and bring him in dead or alive. But because he was old massa's friend, he said, "Why don't you buy the boy's services off?" So old massa took the boat, cat rig we called it, and loaded it with corn and such, and we poled it down to Galveston. The people needed food so much, that load of supplies bought off Massa Tucker from fighting.

After war started, lots of slaves ran off to get to the Yankees. All them in this part headed for the Rio Grande River. The Mexicans rigged up flatboats out in the middle of the river, tied stakes with rope. When the colored people got to the rope they could pull themselves across the rest of the way on those boats. The white folks rode the Mexican side of that river all the time, but plenty of slaves got through anyway.

I waited on lots of soldiers. I had to get smartweed and boil salt water to bathe them in. That helped the rheumatism. Them soldiers had rheumatism so bad from standing day and night in the water.

JAMES CAPE

One day master Bob came to me and said, "Jim, how would you like to join the army?" You see, the war had started. I said to him, "What do I have to do?" And he said, "Tend horses and ride'em." So the first thing I knew, I was in the army away off east from here, somewhere this side of St. Louis and in Tennessee and Arkansas and other places. I went in the army instead of Dr. Carroll.

After I got in the army, it wasn't so much fun, because tending horses and riding wasn't all I did. No, sir, I had to do shooting and to get shot at! One time we stopped the train, took Yankee money, and lots of other things off that train. That was way up the other side of Tennessee.

You've heard of the battle of Independence [Missouri]? That's where we fought three days and nights. I was not tending horses that time. They gave me a rifle and sent me up front fighting, when we weren't running. We did a heap of running, and that suited this nigger. I could do that better'n advance. When the order came to retreat, I was all ready.

I got shot in the shoulder in that fight, and lots of our soldiers got killed, and we lost our supplies, just left it and ran. Another time we fought two days and nights, and the Yankees were bad that time, too, and we had to run through the river. I sure thought I was going to get drowned then. That's the time we tried to get in St. Louis, but the Yankee men stopped us.

JAMES BOYD

I almost forgot to show you my scar. I fought in that freedom war alongside Massa Sanford and got shot. That bullet went through the breast and out the back and kept me six months in the bed. The first battle I was in was at Halifax, in North Carolina. We got the news of freedom when we were at Vicksburg, in Mississippi. Most of us niggers were afraid to say much.

Preely Coleman, age 85

PREELY COLEMAN

During the war the soldiers stopped by on the way to Mansfield
in Louisiana to get something to eat and stay all night, and that's
when we had the races. There was a mulberry tree we'd run to, and
we'd line up, and the soldiers would say, "Now the first one to
slap that tree gets a quarter," and I nearly always got there first. I
made plenty of quarters slapping that old mulberry tree.

So the children got into their heads to fix me because I won all
the quarters. They threw a rope over my head and started dragging me
down the road and down the hill, and I was nigh about choked to
death. My only friend was Billy, and he was fighting, trying to get me
loose. They were going to throw me in the big spring at the foot of
the hill, but we met Capt. Berryman, a white man, and he took his knife
and cut the rope from my neck and took me by the heels and soused
me up and down in the spring till I came to. They never tried to kill me
any more.

NELSON DENSON

Before Texas seceded, Marse Jensen sold us all to Marse Felix Grundy,
and he went to war in General Hardeman's brigade, and I was with
him as bodyguard. When the battle of Mansfield came, I was sixteen
years old. We were camped on the Sabine River, on the Texas side,
and the Yankees were on the other side a little ways. I remember the
night before the battle, how the campfires looked, and it was a quiet
night and the whipperwills were calling in the weeds. We were expecting
an attack and sang to keep cheerful. The Yanks sang the "Battle Cry of
Freedom" when they charged us. They came on and on and, Lord,
how they fought! I stayed close to Marse Grundy, and the rebels won
and took about a thousand Yanks.

MARTIN JACKSON

I was here in Texas when the Civil War was first talked about. I was
here when the war started and followed my young master into it with
the first Texas Cavalry. I was here during reconstruction, after the
war. I was here during the European War, and the second week after the
United States declared war on Germany I enlisted as a cook at Camp
Leon Springs.

This sounds as if I liked the war racket. But, as a matter of fact, I
never wore a uniform—grey coat or khaki coat—or carried a gun, unless
it happened to be one worth saving after some Confederate soldier
got shot. I was official lugger-in of men that got wounded, and might
have been called a Red Cross worker if we had had such a corps
connected with our company. My father was head cook for the battal-

Martin Jackson, age 90

ion and between times I helped him out with the mess. There was some difference in the food served to soldiers in 1861 and 1917.

Just what my feelings were about the war, I have never been able to figure out. I knew the Yanks were going to win, from the beginning I wanted them to win and lick us Southerners, but I hoped they were going to do it without wiping out our company. I'll come back to that in a minute. As I said, our company was the First Texas Cavalry. Col. Buchell [Augustus C. Buchel, who commanded the First Regiment, Texas Cavalry] was our commander. He was a fullblooded German and as fine a man and a soldier as you ever saw. He was killed at the Battle of Marshall [Mansfield] and died in my arms. You may be interested to know that my old master, Alvy Fitzpatrick, was the grandfather of Governor Jim Ferguson.

Lots of colored boys did escape and joined the Union army, and there are plenty of them drawing a pension today. My father was always counseling me. He said every man has to serve God under his own vine and fig tree. He kept pointing out that the war wasn't going to last forever, but that our forever was going to be spent living among Southerners, after they got licked. He would cite examples of how whites would stand flatfooted and fight for the blacks the same as for members of their own family. I knew that all was true, but still I rebelled, from inside me. I think I really was afraid to run away because I thought my conscience would haunt me.

It was in the Battle of Marshall [Mansfield], in Louisiana, that Col. Buchell was shot. I was about three miles from the front, where I had pitched up a kind of first-aid station. I was all alone there. I watched the whole thing. I could hear the shooting and see the firing. I remember standing there thinking the South didn't have a chance. All of a sudden I heard someone. It was a soldier, who was half carrying Col. Buchell in. I didn't do anything for the colonel. He was too far gone. I just held him comfortable, and that was the position he was in when he stopped breathing. That was the worst hurt I got when anybody died. He was a friend of mine. He had had a lot of soldiering before and fought in the Indian War.

Well, the battle of Marshall broke the back of the Texas Cavalry. [Jackson is in error. This battle was actually a minor Confederate victory.] We began straggling back towards New Orleans, and by that time the war was over. The soldiers began to scatter. They were a sorry looking bunch of lost sheep. They didn't know where to go, but most of 'em ended up pretty close to the towns they started from. They were like homing pigeons, with only the instinct to go home, and yet most of them had no home to go to.

KATIE DARLING

I remember that fight at Mansfield like it was yesterday. Massa's field was all torn up with cannon holes and every time a cannon fired, missy went off in a rage. One time when a cannon fired, she said to me, "You little black wench, you niggers aren't going to be free. You're made to work for white folks." About that time she looked up and saw a Yankee soldier standing in the door with a pistol. She said, "Katie, I didn't say anything, did I?" I said, "I'm not telling a lie; you said niggers aren't going to get free."

LAFAYETTE PRICE

In 1861 war commenced, and my mistress died. I was then staying with the Carroll family. The Carrolls were brothers of my owner. Mr. Jim and Mr. Robert were soldiers in the war. Mr. Robert was in the infantry and Mr. Jim they took along to drive. When they were going to Barn Chest, Mr. Robert said to me, "Fay, you go back home and tell ma she need not be uneasy about us because the Yankees are retreating to Nachitoches [Louisiana]." So I drove back but I didn't put up the team. When I was telling her, a big cannon shot overhead—"Boom." She just shook and said, "Oh, Fay, get some corn and throw it to the hogs and go to Chicet." I got some corn and started to get out the crib. They shot another cannon. She said to me, "Go back and give the corn to the pigs." When I put my feet through the crib door, they, shot another shot, and I pulled my feet back. She told me to go back and feed the pigs, but I don't know if I ever did get the corn to the pigs.

Mr. Carroll said that at Mansfield where they were shooting the big guns, the ladies were crying. He told them they needn't cry now, when they were shooting the big guns, they weren't killing men, but when they heard the little guns shoot, then they could start crying, cause that meant that men were getting killed. I don't know if you ever parched popcorn. That's the way the little guns sounded. He said that was when they could begin crying. Our white people [the Confederates] were coming from Shreveport to meet the Yankees from Nachitoches, aiming to Shreveport. If anything was a wonderful consideration, it was then. Mr. Robert Carroll was stood up by a big tree there at Mansfield, and the captain, he said, "Is anybody here that knows the neighborhood?" Here's the thing they wanted to know: When the soldiers started out, they didn't want them to launch out and get mixed up. They sent for Mr. Carroll because he lived about a mile away. He was ordered to stand by the tree, and the captain went by waving a sword, and pretty soon the captain was killed. They kept on fighting and after awhile a soldier came by and asked what he was doing there. He said he had orders to stand there. The soldier said that the captain was killed and for him to go and help with the wounded soldiers. When the big general came from Shreveport and hollered

"Charge," the Yankees got in the corner of a rail fence. They broke right through that old field prairie and 60 men got killed dead before they got across. Next day, coming home, I want to tell you the horses didn't lay on this side or on that side; they just squatted down; they were dead.

One night right where the battle was fought we had to camp. It was raining and sleeting and snowing! I said, "What are you going to do tonight?" Mr. James Carroll said, "We just have to stand where we camp. Just stack the guns and put out what you call the watchman." I said, "Sentinel," and he said, "Yes." They had what you call a relief. They weren't in bed; they were out under a tree in the cold. Every hour they'd walk 'em out along a run way to walk guard. It was a wonderful distressing time. The soldiers had a little song they sang:

Eat when you're hungry,
Drink when you're dry.
If a tree don't kill you,
You'll live till you die.

This was cause they had to stand under trees, and when the Yankees shot cannon, they'd knock off the limbs and tops of trees, and those under the tree might get killed from the falling branches. Another song was:

It was on the eighth of April,
They all remember well,
When fifes and drums were beating,
For us all to march away.

Those 60 men that were killed, they just dug a big hole and put 'em in it and threw dirt on them. I went back after three days, and the bodies had swollen and cracked the ground.

VAN MOORE

When the war broke out, the Union soldiers had a camp not far from us, and I slipped down there when old missy was not looking, cause the soldiers gave me black coffee and sugar which I took to my mammy. I had to walk in the sand up to the knees to get to that camp. Lots more children went, too, but I never saw no cruelness by the soldiers. They gave you sugar in the big bucket, and when you put the hand in it, you could pinch water out of it, cause it was not refined sugar like you get now, but it sure tasted good.

Mammy wrapped me in both the Yankee and Confederate flags,

when I went to that camp, and the soldiers took off the Confederate flag, but I always wore it around the house, cause old missy told me to.

A. C. PRUITT

Just before freedom we moved to Snowball, Texas, which was somewhere close to Cold Springs. They told us they were trying to keep us slaves away from the Yankees. They were everywhere, just like those little black ants that get in the sugar, only they were blue. I was just a little child then, running around in my split shirt tail.

Us children ran down to the rail gate when we saw dust clouds coming and watched the soldiers riding and marching by. They didn't ever do any fighting around us, but there were gunboats down the bayou away, and we could hear the big guns from the other fights. Us little niggers sure liked to wave to them soldiers, and when the men on horses went by, they seemed like they were more enjoying themselves than the others.

ALLEN PRICE

My master thought he was going to escape the worst of the war when he came to Texas, and they were living peaceably the year I was born [1862] raising cotton. There was a gin which my pappy worked in, and they made their own clothes, too, when the Yankees had the Texas ports blockaded so the ships couldn't get in. When they blockaded Galveston, our old master took my pappy for bodyguard and volunteered to help. Finally Gen. Magruder took Galveston from the Yankees with two old cotton steamers which had cotton bales on the decks for breastworks.

The last battle Master Price and my pappy were in was the Battle of Sabine Pass, and the Yankee General, Banks, sent about five thousand troops on transports with gunboats to force a landing. Captain Dick Dowling had seven men to defend that pass, and my pappy helped build breastworks when those Yankees were firing. Captain Dowling ran them Yankees off and took the steamer Clinton and about three hundred and fifty prisoners. My pappy told me some of the captain's men didn't have real guns; they had wooden guns, what they'd call camouflage nowadays.

My pappy helped at the hospital after that battle, and they had it in a hotel and made bandages out of sheets and pillow cases and underwear, and used the rugs and carpets for quilts.

SUSAN ROSS

I just remember I used to see soldiers in blue uniforms walking all

108

John Price and wife Miranda, age about 80

over the country watching how things were going. Massa wanted one
of my brothers to go to war, but he wouldn't, so I saw him buckle my
brother down on a log and whip him with whips, then with hand saws
till when he turned him loose you couldn't tell what he looked like.
My brother left, but I don't know whether he went to war or not.

I remember when the men were going to war, somebody always
came to get them. Lots of them didn't want to go, but they had to.

MARTHA PATTON

I remember seeing the soldiers, but there wasn't any fighting around
us closer than Corpus Christi. One day one of my uncles went to
Corpus Christi. He said, "They have told all the women and children
to get out of town." We heard them shooting bombs. The smoke was
so thick it looked like it was cloudy. The soldiers came through and
took everything they wanted out of the stores. Pretty soon nothing
was left in the stores, and they couldn't get any more.

JOHN PRICE

When the war was breaking out, old massa came by ship to Galveston
up the Trinity River to Liberty by boat to try to save his niggers, but
it wasn't any use. We saw lots of tents out by Liberty, and they said
it was soldiers. I tagged along with the big boys; they sneaked out the
spades and dug holes in the prairie in the knolls. We were planning to
live in them holes in the knolls. When they said the Yankees were coming, I sure was afraid, and I heard the cannon say, "Boom, boom,"
from Galveston to Louisiana. The young white missy, she always sang
the song that went:

We are a band of brothers, native to the soil,
Fighting for our liberty, with treasure, blood, and
*   toil,*

And when our rights were threatened, the cry rose
*   far and near,*
Hurrah for the Bonnie Blue flag that bears the
*   single star.*

JULIA FRANCIS DANIELS

The soldiers used to pass, and all the whooping and hollering and
carrying on, you never heard the likes! They hollered, "Who-o-o-o, old
man Denman, how's your chickens?" And they chunked and threw
at them till they crippled them up and put them in their bags for cooking. Old man Denman cursed at them something powerful.

110

My sister Mandy and me were down in the woods a good far piece from the house, and we kept hearing a noise. My brother came down and found me and said, "Come get your dinner." When I got there, dinner was on the gate post, and he said there were soldiers in the woods, and they had been persecuting an old woman on a mule. She was a nigger woman. I got so scared I couldn't eat my dinner. I hadn't got any heart for victuals. My brother said, "Wait for pa, he's coming with the mule, and he'll hide you out." I got on the mule in front of pa, and we passed through the soldiers, and they grabbed at me and said, "Give me the gal, give me the gal." Pa said I fainted plumb away.

We heard guns shooting around and about all the time. Seems like they fought every time they got a chance. Old man Denman's boy got killed, and two of my sisters were his property, and they didn't know what to do because they had to be somebody's property, and there was no one to inherit them. They had to go to the auction, but old man Denman said not to fret. At the auction the man said, "Going high, going low, going mighty slow, a little while to go. Bid 'em in, bid 'em in. The sun is high, the sun is hot and we got to get home tonight." An old friend of old man Denman's hollered out what he'd pay for them.

HARRISON BOYD

The soldiers confiscated lots of corn from massa, and some more owners in Rusk County piled corn up in a big heap and made me go mind it till the rest of the soldiers got there. I was sitting atop that corn pile, me and my bulldog, and the General rode up. My dog growled, and I made him hush. The General man said to me, "Boy, you are excused now, go on home." I got to a fence and looked back, and that General was hewing him a horse trough out of a log. The soldiers came in droves and set up their camp. I sat on a stump and watched them pass. They stayed three, four days till the corn was all fed up.

While they camped there, they caught chickens. They had a fishing pole and line and hook. They put a grain of corn on the hook and pitched the hook out among the chickens. When a chicken swallowed the corn, they'd jerk up the line with that chicken and ride off.

MILLIE FORWARD

When the soldiers went to the war, every man took a slave to wait on him and take care of his camp and cook. After the end of the war, when the soldiers had gone home, don't know how many Yankees passed through Jasper, but it sounded like the roar of a storm coming. Every officer had his wife riding right by his side. Their wives came to go home with them. There were thousands of bluecoats, riding two abreast.

111

FELIX HAYWOOD

It's a funny thing how folks always want to know about the war. The war wasn't so great as folks suppose. Sometimes you didn't know it was going on. It was the ending of it that made the difference. That was when we all woke up that something had happened. Oh, we knew what was going on in it all the time, because old man Gudlow went to the post office every day, and we knew. We had papers in them days just like now.

But the war didn't change anything. We saw guns, and we saw soldiers, and one member of master's family, Colmin Gudlow, was gone fighting—somewhere. But he didn't get shot no place but one—that was in the big toe. Then there were neighbors who went off to fight. Some of them didn't want to go, but they were taken away. I'm thinking lots of them pretended to want to go as soon as they had to go.

The ranch went on just like it always had before the war. Church went on. Old ma Johnson, the preacher, saw to it church went on. The kids didn't know what was happening. They played marbles, see-saw, and rode. I had old buster, an ox, and he took me about plenty good as a horse. Nothing was different.

ABRAM SELLS

Remember the war? Course I do. I remember how some of them marched off in their uniforms, looking so grand, and how some of them hid out in the wood to keep from looking so grand. There was lots of talking about fighting, and rubbing and scrubbing the old shotgun. The oldest niggers were sitting around the fire late in the night, stirring the ashes with the poker and raking out the roast taters. They were smoking the old corncob pipe and homemade tobacco and whispering right low and quiet about what they were going to do and where they were going to when Mister Lincoln, he turned them free.

The more they talked, the more I got scared that the nigger was going to get set free and wondering what I was going to do if they were. No, I guess I don't want to live back in those times no more, but I sure saw lots of niggers not doing as well as they did when they were slaves and not having near as much to eat.

112

 CHAPTER IX

FREE AT LAST

FELIX HAYWOOD

Hallelujah broke out—
Abe Lincoln freed the nigger,
With the gun and the trigger,
And I ain't going to get whipped no more.
I got my ticket,
Leaving the thicket,
And I'm heading for the Golden shore.

Soldiers, all of a sudden were everywhere—coming in bunches, crossing, and walking, and riding. Everyone was singing. We were all walking on golden clouds. Hallelujah!

Union forever,
Hurrah, boys, hurrah!
Although I may be poor,
I'll never be a slave—
Shouting the battle cry of freedom.

Everybody went wild. We all felt like heroes, and nobody had made us that way but ourselves. We were free. Just like that, we were free. It didn't seem to make the whites mad, either. They went right on giving us food just the same. Nobody took our homes, but right off colored folks started on the move. They seemed to want to get closer to freedom, so they knew what it was—like it was a place or a city.

We knew freedom was on us, but we didn't know what was to come with it. We thought we were going to get rich like the white folks. We thought we were going to be richer than the white folks, because we were stronger and knew how to work, and the whites didn't, and we didn't have to work for them any more. But it didn't turn out that way. We soon found out that freedom could make folks proud but it didn't make them rich.

SUSAN ROSS

When my oldest brother heard we were free, he gave a whoop, ran, and jumped a high fence, and told mammy good-bye. Then he grabbed me up and hugged and kissed me and said, "Brother is gone, don't expect you'll ever see me any more." I don't know where he went, but I never did see him again.

ANNIE ROW

During the war Marster Charley cussed everything and everybody, and we had to watch out and keep out of his way. After two years he got a letter from Marster Billy and he said he would be home soon and that John was killed. Missy started crying and marster jumped up and started cursing the war, and he picked up the hot poker and said, "Free the nigger, will they. I'll free them." And he hit my mammy on the neck, and she started moaning and crying and dropped to the floor. There they were, the missy a-moaning, my mammy a moaning, and the marster cussing as loud as he could. He took the gun off the rack and started for the field where the niggers were working. My sister and I saw that, and we started running and screaming, because we had brothers and sisters in the field. But the good Lord took a hand in that mess, and the marster hadn't gone far in the field when he dropped all of a sudden. The death set in on the marster, and the niggers came running to him. He couldn't talk or move, and they toted him in the house. The doctor came, and the next day marster died.

Then Marster Billy came home, and he broke up the place with the freedom for the niggers. Most of them left as soon as they could.

The missy got very condescending after freedom. The women were in the spinning house, and we expected another whipping and scolding, cause that was the usual doing when she came. She came in and said, "Good morning, women," and she never said such before. She said she would pay wages to all who stayed and told how good she would treat them. But my pappy came and took us over to the widow Perry's land to work for shares.

After that, the missy found Marster Billy dead in the shed, with his throat cut and the razor beside him. There was a piece of paper

114

saying he did not care to live because the niggers were free and they were all broken up.

MOLLY HARRELL

Everybody talked about freedom and hoped to get free before they died. I remember the first time the Yankees passed by, my mother lifted me up on the fence. They used to pass by with bags on the mules and fill them with stuff from the houses. They went in the barn and helped themselves. They went in the stables and turned out the white folks' horses and ran off what they didn't take for themselves.

Then one night I remember just as well, me and my mother were in the cabin getting ready to go to bed, when we heard somebody call her. We listened, and the overseer whispered under the door and told my mother that she was free but not to tell anybody. I don't know why he did it. He always liked mother, so I guess he did it for her. The master read us the paper right after that and said we were free.

Me and my mother left right off and went to Palestine. Most everybody else went with us. We all walked down the road singing and shouting to beat the band.

ANDREW GOODMAN

When Marse Bob came home, he sent for all the slaves. He was sitting in a yard chair, all tuckered out, and shook hands all around, and said he was glad to see us. Then he said, "I've got something to tell you. You are just as free as I am. You don't belong to nobody but yourselves. We went to the war and fought, and the Yankees done whipped us, and they say the niggers are free. You can go where you want to go, or you can stay here, just as you like. He couldn't help but cry.

The niggers cried but didn't know much what Marse Bob meant. They were sorry about the freedom because they didn't know where to go, and they'd always depended on old Marse to look after them. Three families went to get farms for themselves, but the rest just stayed on for hands on the old place.

The Federals had been coming by, even before Old Marse came home. They all came by, carrying their little buckets, and if they were walking they'd look in the stables for a horse or mule, and they just took what they wanted of corn or livestock. They did the same after Marse Bob came home. He just said, "Let them go their way, because that's what they're going to do anyway." We were scarder of them than we were of the devil. But they spoke right kindly to us colored folks. They said, "If you got a good master and want to stay, well you can do that, but now you can go where you want to, cause there ain't nobody going to stop you."

The niggers couldn't hardly get used to the idea. When they wanted to leave the place, they still went up to the big house for a pass. They just couldn't understand about the freedom. Old Marse or Missus said "You don't need no pass. All you got to do is just take your foot in your hand and go."

JAMES BROWN

The day before master gave us freedom, he said to us, "I want all you niggers to come to the front of the house Sunday morning." We were there, and he was standing on the gallery, holding a paper in his hand and reading. There were tears in his eyes and some dropped on the paper. I had tears in my eyes, too; most of them did. When he was done reading, he said, "You darkies are as free as I am. You can go or you can stay. Those that stay till the crops are laid by, I'll give $5.00 a month."

Then he took the little niggers and said, "Those little fellows whose mammies I've sold will stay with me till they are 21 years old. You little fellows, I know your age, and I'll give you the statement."

ELSIE REECE

Then surrender came, and Massa Jim read the long paper. He said, "I'll explain to you. It's the order from the government which makes it against the law to keep you as slaves." You should have seen those colored folks. They just shook. Their faces were as long as their arms, and so pestered they didn't know what to say or do.

Massa never said another word and walked away. The colored folks said, "Where are we going to live?" "What are we going to do?" Uncle John said, "When do we have to go?" Then massa laughed heartily and said they could stay for wages or work on halves. Well, sir, there were a bunch of happy colored folks after they learned they could stay and work.

JAMES HAYES

Three days after the celebration, the master called all the slaves in the house and said, "You are all free, free as I am." He told us we could go if we wanted to. None of us knew what to do; there was no place to go, and why would we want to go and leave good folks like master? His place was our home. So we asked him if we could stay, and he said, "You can stay as long as you want to, and I can keep you." We all stayed till he died, about a year after that.

WILLIAM MOORE

One day I was in a 'simmon tree in the middle of a little pond eating

116

Walter Rimm, age 80

'simmons, and my sister, Mandy, came running. She said, "We niggers are free." I looked over to the house and saw the niggers piling their little bunch of clothes and things outside their cabins. Then mammy came running with some other niggers, and mammy was head runner. I climbed down out of that tree and ran to meet her. She said Marse Tom had told her he was going to keep me and pay her for it. She was scared. I would have to stay if I wanted to or not, and she begged me not to.

We got up to the house and all the niggers were standing there with their little bundles on their heads, and they all said, "Where are we going?"

Mammy said, "I don't know where you are all going, but me, myself, am to go to Miss Mary's." So all the niggers got in the cart with Mammy and went to Miss Mary's. She met us by the back door and said, "Come in, Jane, and all you children and all the rest of you. You can see my door is open and my smokehouse door is open to you, and I'll bed you down till we figure a way for you."

We all cried and sang and prayed and were so excited we didn't eat any supper, though Mammy stirred up some victuals.

It wasn't long before we found places to work. Miss Mary found us a place with a fine white man, and we worked on shares and drifted around to some other places and lived in Corsicana for a while and bought Mammy a little house, and she died there.

WALTER RIMM

One day I saw massa sitting on the gallery, and his face was all screwed up. He said, "Go get your mammy and everybody." I went a-flying. My shirt tail didn't hit my back till I told everybody. Massa was crying, and he read a paper and said, "You are as free as I am. What you going to do?" Mammy said, "I'm staying right here." But next morning pappy borrowed an ox team to take our stuff away. We went about sixty miles and stayed about six months, and took a place where we could make a crop.

JULIA FRANCIS DANIELS

I was a woman grown when the war came to an end. I had my first baby when I was fourteen. One day my sister called me and said, "They're fought out, and they've been surrendering and aren't going to fight no more." That dusk old man Denman called all us niggers together and stood on his steps and made his speech. "Men and women, you are as free as I am. You are free to go where you want, but I am begging you to stay by me till we get the crops laid by." Then he said, "Study it over before you give me your answer. I have always tried as my duty to be fair to you."

Louise Mathews, age 83

The men talked it over a-twixt themselves and concluded to stay. They said we might as well stay there as go somewhere else, and we had no money and no place to go.

LOUISE MATHEWS

I remember that surrender day. He called us round him. I can see him now, like I watch him come to the yard with his hands clasped behind him and his head lowered. I know what he said, "I love every one of you. You've been faithful, but I have to give you up. I hate to do it, not because I don't want to free you but because I don't want to lose you all." We saw the tears in his eyes.

C. B. MCRAY

When freedom was declared, Miss Mary called us niggers into the parlor and then Marster McRay came and told us we were free. He advised them to work around Jasper where they knew people, and said if any wanted to stay with him to please rise up. Every person rose up. So they all stayed with him for a time. After a while he began to rent and cultivate different plantations, and there treatment was not so good, so they began to become dissatisfied and pulled loose.

JOHN CRAWFORD

One morning the judge sent word down by the cook for nobody to go to the fields that day. We all went up to the big house and the judge got up to make a speech. But he was too choked up to talk. He hated to lose his slaves, I reckon. So his son-in-law had to say, "You folks are now free and can go where you want to. You can stay here and pick cotton and get fifty cents the hundred." But only two families stayed. The rest pulled out.

ISAAC MARTIN

When freedom came and the proclamation was read and the old master told them they were free and didn't have no master any more, some of the slaves cried. He told them, "I don't want any of you to leave. I'll give you $8.00 a month." All the old folks stayed and helped gather that crop. It sure grieved old master, and he didn't live long after they took his slaves away from him. Well, it just killed him, that's all. I remember the Yankees on that day they set to read the proclamation. They were going around in their blue uniforms and a big sword hanging at their side. That was a curiosity to those niggers.

JOHN SNEED

I well remember the day freedom was declared. We had the tearing

down dinner that day. The niggers bellered and cried and didn't want
to leave massa. He talked to us and said as long as he lived we'd be
cared for, and we were. There were lots of springs on his place, and
the married niggers picked out a spring, and Massa Doctor gave them
stuff to put up the cabin by that spring, and they took what they had
in the quarters. They wanted to move from those slave quarters but
not too far from massa. They came to the big house for flour and meal
and meat and such till massa died. He willed every last one of his slaves
something. Most of them got a cow and a horse and a pig and some
chickens. My mammy got two cows and a pair of horses and a wagon
and 70 acres of land.

ABE LIVINGSTON

News of freedom came about 9 or 10 o'clock on a Tuesday morning.
Most of us went home and stayed there till next Monday. Then the
Yankees came and told us we were free. About 80 of them came and
they sure laughed a lot, like they were glad war was through. Seems
like they were more for eating than anything else, and they stole the
good horses. They took everything to eat, and 40 big gobblers, and
they ate the hogs and beeves, too. How them Yankees could eat. I
never saw anything like it.

SUSAN MERRITT

I heard about freedom in September, and they were picking cotton
and a white man rode up to massa's house on a big, white horse,
and the houseboy told massa a man wanted to see him, and he
hollered, "Alight, stranger." It was a government man, and he had
a big book and a bunch of papers and said why massa hadn't
turned the niggers loose. Massa said he was trying to get the crop
out, and he told massa to have the slaves in. Uncle Steven blew
the cow horn which they used to call to eat, and all the niggers
came running, cause the horn meant "Come to the big house, quick."
That man read that paper telling us we were free, but massa made
us work several months after that. He said we got 20 acres land and
a mule, but we didn't get it.

Lots of niggers were killed after freedom, cause the slaves in
Harrison County were turned loose right at freedom, and those in
Rusk County weren't. But they heard about it and ran away to
freedom in Harrison County, and their owners had them bushwhacked,
that's shot down. You could see lots of niggers hanging to trees in
Sabine bottom right after freedom, cause they caught them swimming
across the Sabine River and shot them. There sure are going to be lots
of souls crying against them in Judgement!

Anderson and Minerva Edwards, ages 93 and 87

LIZA JONES

When the Yankees came to see if they had turned us loose, I was a nine year old nigger gal. They promenaded up to the gate and their drum said a-dr-um-m-m-m, and the man in the blue uniform he got down to open the gate. Old massa he saw them coming, and he ran in the house and grabbed the gun. When he came hustling down off the gallery, my daddy came running. He saw that old massa was too mad to know what he was doing, so quicker than a chicken could fly he grabbed that gun and wrestled it out of old massa's hands. Then he pushed old massa into the smokehouse and locked the door. He didn't do that to be mean, but he wanted to keep old massa out of trouble. Old massa knew that, but he beat on the door and yelled, but it didn't get opened till those Yankees had gone.

ANDERSON EDWARDS

Before the war massa didn't ever say much about slavery, but when he heard we were free, he cussed and said, "God never did intend to free niggers," and he cussed till he died. But he didn't tell us we were free till a whole year after we were, but one day a bunch of Yankee soldiers came riding by, and massa and missy hid out. The soldiers walked into the kitchen, and mammy was churning, and one of them kicked the churn over and said, "Get out, you're just as free as I am." Then they ransacked the house and broke out all the window lights, and when they left it looked like a storm had hit that house. Massa came back from hiding, and that's when he started on a cussing spree which lasted as long as he lived.

ELI DAVISON

After I was traded off, my new massa wasn't so good to me. He thought all the time the South would win that war, and he treated us mean. He kept telling us a black nigger never would be free. When it came, he said to us, "Well, you black _____, you are just as free as I am." He turned us loose with nothing to eat and almost no clothes. He said if he got up next morning, and found a nigger on his place, he'd horsewhip him.

JOHN BATES

My Uncle Bent he could read the Bible, and he always told us some day we'd be free, and Master Harry laughed, haw, haw, haw, and he said, "Hell, no, you'll never be free; you haven't got sense enough to make a living if you were free." Then he took the Bible away from Uncle Bent and said it put bad ideas in his head, but Uncle got another Bible and hid it, and master never found it out.

When the news came in that we were free, Master Harry never called us like everybody else did their slaves; we had to go up and ask him about it. He came out on the front gallery and said we were free and turned around and went in the house without another word. We all sure felt sorry for him for the way he acted, and hated to leave him, but we wanted to go. We knew he wasn't able to give us anything, so we began to scatter, and then about ten or fifteen days later Master Harry died. I think he just grieved himself to death, all his trouble coming on him at once.

MANDY HADNOT

When freedom came my mother and me paid no attention to it. We stayed right on the place. Pretty soon my mother died, and I just took up her chores. One day I was making a bonfire in the yard and caught my dress on fire. The whole side of my left leg almost burned off. Mistress was so little she couldn't lift, but she finally got me to bed. There I stayed for a long, long time, and she waited on me hand and foot. She made linseed poultice and kept the burn greased good. Most times she left all the work standing in the middle of the floor and read the Bible and prayed for me to get healed up and not suffer. She cried right along with me when I cried, cause I hurt so.

My old mistress paid me money right along after freedom, but I was too close to spend any. Then when I decided to marry Bob Thomas, she helped me get a hope chest. I bought goods for sheets and table covers, and one nice Sunday set of dishes.

We married right in the parlor of the master's house. The white man preacher married us, and mistress gave me away. Old mistress helped me make my wedding dress out of white cotton. I had pretty, long, black hair and a veil with a ribbon around the front. The wedding feast was strawberry ice cream and yellow cake. Old mistress gave me my bedstead, one of her prettiest ones, and the set of dishes and glasses we ate the wedding dinner out of. My husband gave me the traveling dress, but I never used that dress for three weeks, though, cause old mistress cried so when I had to leave that I stayed for three weeks after I married.

She was all alone in the big house, and I think it broke her heart. I hadn't been gone to the sawmill town very long when she sent for me. I went to see her and took a peach pie, cause I loved her, and I knew that's what she liked better than anything. She was sick, and she said, "Mandy, this is the last time we're going to see each other, cause I ain't going to get well. You be a good girl and try to get through the world that way." Then she asked me to say the Lord's prayer with her just like she always made me say it for a night prayer when I was a little gal. I never saw her no more.

124

ISABELLA BOYD

When we all got free, they were a long time letting us know. They wanted to get through with the corn and cotton before they let the hands loose. There were people from other plantations who said, "Niggers, you're free and here you are working." We said, "No, the government will tell us when we're free." We were working one day when somebody from Master Grissom's place came by and told us we were free, and we stopped working. They told us to go on working, and the boss man he came up, and he said he was going to knock us off the fence if we didn't go back to work. Mistress came out and said, "Aren't you going to make them niggers go to work?" He sent her back in the house, and he called for the carriage, and said he was going to town to see what the government was going to. Next day he came back and said, "Well, you're just as free as I am."

TEMPIE CUMMINS

Mother was working in the house, and she cooked, too. She said she used to hide in the chimney corner and listen to what the white folks said. When freedom was declared, master wouldn't tell them, but mother, she heard him telling mistress that the slaves were free, but they didn't know it, and he was not going to tell 'em till he had made another crop or two. When mother heard that, she said she slipped out of the chimney corner and cracked her heels together four times and shouted, "I's free, I's free." Then she ran to the field, against master's will, and told all the other slaves, and they quit work. Then she ran away, and in the night she slipped into the big ravine near the house and had them bring me to her. Master, he came out with his gun and shot at mother, but she ran down the ravine and got away with me.

MATTIE GILMORE

It ain't so long before a paper came to make us free. Some of the slaves were laughing and some crying, and it was a funny place to be. Marse Barrow asked my stepma to stay and cook and he'd pay her some money for it. We stayed four or five years. Marse Barrow gave each of his slaves something when they were freed. Lots of masters put them out without a thing. But the trouble with most niggers, they had never done no managing and didn't know how. The niggers suffered from the war even if they did get freedom from it.

JULIA MALONE

I remember being left in the nursery while my mammy worked in the fields. One night she went to the river to wash clothes. She had to wash after dark, and she was washing, and a nigger slave snuck up on her and hit her on the neck, and it was the death of her. So that woman whom mammy always lived with took care of me then and when freedom came she moved to town, but massa wouldn't allow her to take me. I stayed with him and ran errands, while I was not fanning the new baby. They had six while I was there. I fanned them till I dropped asleep, and that called for a whipping.

My foster mammy came out and asked massa to let her have me, but he wouldn't do that. But she put one over on him finally and got me anyway. He was gone and missus was gone, and I had to stay home alone with the last baby, and a man and woman, who were slaves on the place before surrender, came by in a wagon and told me to jump in. They took me to my foster mammy, and she moved and wouldn't allow me outside, so massa couldn't ever find me.

ANDY J. ANDERSON

Then surrender was announced and master told us we were free. When that took place, it was about one o'clock by sun. I said to myself, I won't be here long. But I had not realized what I was in for till after I'd started, but I couldn't turn back, for that meant whipping or danger from the patrollers. There I was and kept on going. No nigger was supposed to be off the master's place without a pass, so I traveled at night and hid out during the day. I stayed in the brush and got water from the creeks, but didn't get much to eat. Twice I was sure those patrollers were passing while I was hiding.

I was 21 years old then, but it was the first time I'd gone any place except to the neighbors, so I was worried about the right way to Master Haley's place. But the morning of the third day I came to the place, and I was so hungry and tired and scared for fear Master Haley was not home from the army yet. So I found my pappy, and he hid me in his cabin till a week passed, and then luck came to me when Master Haley came home. He came at night and the next morning that Delbridge [the overseer] was sent off the place, because Master Haley saw the niggers were all gaunt and lots had run off, and the fields were not plowed right, and only half the sheep and everything was left. So master said to that Delbridge, "There are no words that can explain what you've done. Get off my place before I smash you."

Then I could come out from my pappy's cabin, and the old master was glad to see me, and he let me stay till freedom was ordered. That was the happiest time in my life, when I got back to Master Haley.

JOHN McCOY

Freedom wasn't no difference I knew of. I worked for Marse John just

126

the same for a long time. He said one morning, "John, you can go out in the field if you want to, or you can get out if you want to, cause the government says you are free. If you want to work I'll feed you and give you clothes but can't give you any money. I haven't got any." Humph, I didn't know what money was, anyhow, but I knew I'd get plenty of victuals, so I stayed till old marse died and old miss got shut off the place.

APPENDIX

WILL ADAMS, born in 1857 in Harrison County, Texas, lived alone in Marshall when interviewed in 1937. His only income came from a $13 a month pension.

WILLIAM M. ADAMS had spent 93 years in Texas. He was born in San Jacinto County and spent his life working in grocery stores, punching cattle, farming, and preaching. He moved to Fort Worth in 1902 and still lived there when interviewed.

ANDY J. ANDERSON, 94 years old when interviewed in Fort Worth, was a native of Williamson County, Texas.

STEARLIN ARNWINE was born near Jacksonville, Texas, 84 years before an interviewer recorded his story six miles west of there in 1937.

SARAH ASHLEY, a native of Mississippi, was carried to Texas as a child. She was 93 when her recollections were recorded at Goodrich, Texas.

JOHN BARKER, 84, was born near Cincinnati, Ohio, and lived in Missouri before coming to Texas. He and his wife resided in a neat cottage near Houston when interviewed.

HARRIET BARRETT told an interviewer who visited her Palestine home that she was born in Walker County, Texas, in 1851.

JOHN BATES was born at Little Rock, Arkansas, in 1854, and moved with his mother and master to Limestone County, Texas, while still very young. In 1937 he lived in Corsicana, supported by his children and an old age pension.

HARRISON BECKETT didn't remember her age but knew she grew up in San Augustine, Texas. Interviewers found her in Beaumont, where they noted a genial smile and a tendency to coin her own words.

CHARLOTTE BEVERLY was born in Montgomery County, Texas, and 90 years later lived with one of her children between Cleveland and Shepherd. Most of her life had been spent within 60 miles of Houston.

FRANCIS BLACK, born in Grand Bluff, Mississippi, in 1857, was taken to a slave market in New Orleans and later sold in Jefferson, Texas. Interviewers located her living at the Ragland Old Folks Home in Texarkana where they learned that she had been blind for a year.

HARRISON BOYD, 87, was born in Rusk County and interviewed in Harrison County, Texas. His memory was poor, and he recalled a few incidents.

ISABELLA BOYD, whose age was unknown, was born in Virginia and moved to Texas before the Civil War. She told her story in Beaumont.

JAMES BOYD, who was about 100 years old, was born in an Indian hut at Phantom Valley, Oklahoma. Later he lived near Waco, before moving to Itasca, where he was interviewed.

MONROE BRACKINS came to Medina County, Texas, in 1855 at the age of two from his birthplace in Mississippi. Interviewers found him living in Hondo, Texas.

WES BRADY, 88, was born just north of Marshall and spent his entire life in Harrison County, Texas.

JACOB BRANCH, a Louisiana native, was sold by a Texas planter while still a baby. Interviewers found him at Double Bayou, near Beaumont, 86 years later. They noted that he was especially spry for his age.

JAMES BROWN, was born in Bell County, Texas, in 1853; he had been taken to Waco while still an infant. Questioners in July, 1937, learned that he had been blind for 12 years and had no living relations. His only income came from a $14 a month pension.

MARTHA SPENCE BUNTON, 81, was a native of Murphreesboro, Tennessee, but moved to Texas with her mother and four sisters before the Civil War. She was interviewed at a home six miles east of Austin.

JAMES CAPE, who said he was over 100 years old, was born on a ranch in southeast Texas and spent most of his youth working as a cowboy. In 1937 he lived in a dilapidated shack in the rear of the Fort Worth stockyards.

RICHARD CARRUTHERS, 100, was born in Memphis, Tennessee, and moved to Bastrop County, Texas, as a child. He later lived in Acres Homes, a black settlement eight miles from Houston.

JACK CAUTHERN, 85, was born near Austin and told his story in San Angelo.

AMOS CLARK was born in Washington County, Texas, in 1841. Interviewers found him residing in Waco.

PREELY COLEMAN remembered nothing of his early life in South Carolina, for he moved to Texas when a month old. He lived in Tyler when interviewed 85 years later.

ANDREW (SMOKEY) COLUMBUS told questioners who met him in Marshall that he was born 78 years earlier south of Linden, Texas.

LAURA CORNISH, 85, was born near Dayton, Texas. When interviewers visited her in Houston, they found that she had a poor memory but made an effort to recall everything she could about slavery.

JOHN CRAWFORD, born at Manor, spent his entire 81 years in Travis County and was living with a daughter in Austin when interviewed.

GREEN CUMBY was a native of Henderson, Texas. At age 86 he lived with a daughter in Abilene.

TEMPIE CUMMINS didn't know her age, but she recalled her birthplace was Brookeland, Texas. Interviewers found her living alone in a weather-beaten shack in the slum section of Jasper.

ADELINE CUNNINGHAM, 85, was born in Lavaca County near Hallettsville, Texas. Questioners who recorded her recollections in San Antonio described her as "tall, spare, and firmly erect, with fiery brown eyes which snap when she recalls the slave days."

JULIA FRANCIS DANIELS, 89, was born in Georgia and came to Texas before the Civil War. She lived with a daughter in Dallas when interviewed. Although unable to recall names and dates, she was willing to provide an unusually detailed account of slave life.

KATIE DARLING grew up in Marshall where she still lived in a three-room shack 88 years later.

CAREY DAVENPORT was a retired Methodist minister who was born and reared in Waller County, Texas. At age 83 he lived with his wife in Anahuac. Interviewers found that he was still sturdy and spent much of his time fishing.

CAMPBELL DAVIS, 85, was a native of Harrison County, Texas. In 1937, he lived with a nephew near Karnack, supported by a $12 monthly pension.

ELI DAVISON grew up in Dunbar, West Virginia, where he was born in 1844. Fourteen years later he moved to Madison County, Texas, where he still lived with a son when interviewed.

NELSON DENSON, 90, a native of Arkansas, resided in Waco when interviewers met him. He had a poor memory and provided little information.

WILLIS EASTER told interviewers who came to her Waco home of her birth 85 years earlier at Nacogdoches. Her major interest was the supernatural world of ghosts and conjuremen.

ANDERSON and MINERVA EDWARDS, 93 and 87 years old respectively, were born on adjoining plantations in Rusk County. After the Civil War they married, moved to Harrison County, and raised sixteen children. Interviewers found the couple living in a small but comfortable house near Marshall.

MARY KINCHEON EDWARDS, who lived near Austin, claimed to be 127 years old, and although interviewers could not verify her statements, they agreed that she was very old. She was born in Louisiana and came to Texas before the Civil War.

JOHN ELLIS was born in 1852 near Cleburne, Texas, and interviewed in San Angelo, where he lived alone. He was still very active.

BETTY FARROW, 90, was raised in Patrick County, Virginia, and brought to Texas before the Civil War.

SARAH FORD did not know her age, but knew she was born near West Columbia, Texas. She was interviewed at her Houston home.

MILLIE FORWARD was born in Jasper in 1842 and lived there with her son 95 years later. She had been blind for fifteen years and had great difficulty hearing.

ROSANNA FRAZIER, 90, was born in Mississippi. Interviewers visiting her in Beaumont found that she had a poor memory and could provide little information.

MATTIE GILMORE, whom interviewers estimated to be about 90, was born in Alabama and brought to Texas during the Civil War. In 1937 she lived in a cabin in Corsicana.

ANDREW GOODMAN, 97, was born near Birmingham, Alabama, but raised in Smith County, Texas, where his master moved when Goodman was still a boy. He told of his life to questioners visiting his Dallas home.

MANDY HADNOT, a small, frail woman, could not pinpoint her birthdate but knew it occurred near Cold Springs, Texas. She lived with her husband in Woodville when interviewed.

WILLIAM HAMILTON didn't know when or where he was born, but he vividly recalled his early life in bondage. Questioners found him living in Fort Worth.

MOLLY HARRELL, who was born near Palestine, recalled having been about 7 when freedom came. She lived in Galveston in 1937.

ANN HAWTHORNE, about 85, was born in Jasper County, where she still lived when interviewed in 1937. Questioners described her as a "generous" woman with snow-white hair fixed in pigtails and wrapped in black string. She had a deep voice and a jovial manner.

JAMES HAYES, 101, was born in Shelby County near Marshall, Texas. At the time of the interview he lived on a green slope overlooking the Trinity River in Moser Valley, a Negro settlement north of Fort Worth. He was alert, stood erect, and generally very active for his age.

FELIX HAYWOOD told interviewers at his San Antonio home that he was born in St. Hedwig, Bexar County, 92 years before.

PHOEBE HENDERSON, 105, came to Texas from her Georgia birthplace in 1859. She later lived with a daughter east of Marshall.

TOM HOLLAND, who thought he was about 97, was born in Waller County and continued living for many years near the old plantation. Interviewers talked to him in Madisonville.

ELIZA HOLMAN was born near Clinton, Mississippi; she came to Texas in 1861 and settled near Decatur. Years later in Fort Worth she related her experiences.

BILL HOMER, 87, grew up near Shreveport, Louisiana; he came to Texas in 1860. Interviewers found him living with his wife in Fort Worth.

LIZZIE HUGHES, who was blind by 1937, was born 89 years earlier in Nacogdoches. She was interviewed near Marshall.

MOSES HURSEY, a preacher with delusions of grandeur, was 82 years old. A native of Louisiana, he was brought to Texas soon after the Civil War.

WASH INGRAM, 93, came to Texas from his native Richmond, Virginia, and lived for many years near Carthage. He was interviewed at Marshall.

MARTIN JACKSON was described as possibly the only Negro living in 1937 who had served in both the Civil War and World War I. At age 90 he recalled his birth in Victoria County, Texas. Interviewers noted that although blind he had an uncommonly clear mind and spoke "with no Negro colloquialisms and almost no dialect."

NANCY JACKSON, about 105, came to Panola County, Texas, from Tennessee when she was three years old. In 1937 she lived with a daughter several miles outside Tatum, Texas.

AUNTIE THOMAS JOHNS was born in Burleson 73 years before an interviewer talked with her in Cleburne. She was too young to remember anything about slavery but related stories she had heard from her mother and husband.

SPENCE JOHNSON, who was presumed to be in his 80's, was born on the Choctaw reserve in the Indian Territory. He was later stolen, sold at a Shreveport, Louisiana market, and finally taken to a plantation on the Texas-Louisiana state line. Interviewers met him in Waco.

HARRIET JONES, 93, was taken to Texas from her native North Carolina as a young girl. She was interviewed in Clarksville, where she lived with a granddaughter.

LEWIS JONES told questioners in Fort Worth that he was born on a Colorado River plantation in Fayette County, Texas, 86 years earlier.

LIZA JONES was 81 years old. As she sat in a backless chair smoking a pipe, she told of her birth near Liberty, Texas, and subsequent life as a slave and freedman. She lived at Beaumont in 1937.

LIZZIE JONES, 86, was born in Harrison County, Texas, and interviewed near Karnack.

NANCY KING was born in 1840 in Upshur County, Texas. Before the Civil War she had married and given birth to a child. In 1937 she lived in Marshall with a daughter.

SILVIA KING, who was probably near 100 years old, was born in Morocco and lived in France before coming to Texas. Her interview took place in Marlin.

UNCLE CINTO LEWIS, who was thought to be about 101, was born in Fort Bend County near Richmond, Texas. Questioners found Lewis living in a cabin which had been part of the slave quarters in an ante-bellum plantation.

HAGAR LEWIS told interviewers in her El Paso home that she was born near Tyler 83 years earlier. A son who was an electrical engineer in New York City supported her in 1937.

HENRY LEWIS showed his 102 years when interviewers met him in Beaumont. The Jefferson County, Texas, native had to strain his vocal cords to talk at all and had a very poor memory.

LUCY LEWIS, the wife of Cinto Lewis, did not know her age, but she was born at Pleasant Grove, Texas. She and her husband lived in a cabin furnished with a huge fourposter bed and some chairs. Pots, pans, kettles, and jugs covered the walls. Both husband and wife were almost blind.

ABE LIVINGSTON, 83, was born in Jasper County and interviewed at Beaumont. His interview was extremely brief.

JULIA MALONE, 79, was born on a plantation near Lockhart, Texas. Interviewers found her living in Fort Worth.

ADELINE MARSHALL did not know her age, but interviewers thought her to be very old. Born in South Carolina, she came to Texas as a baby and lived in Houston when questioned.

ISAAC MARTIN's age was not given, but he was described as "quite black" with close-cut hair and gray whiskers. The Montgomery County, Texas, native, sat in a rocker under a shade tree near his Veth home for the interview. His feet were bare and his trouser legs rolled up to keep cool.

LOUISE MATHEWS, 83, didn't indicate her birthplace, but she was apparently raised in east Texas. Questioners found her living alone in Fort Worth.

HIRAM MAYES, 75, was born in Double Bayou, Texas, and interviewed near the rambling house outside Beaumont he later shared with two daughters. The questioner commented that "native intelligence gleams in his deepest eyes, but his speech shows that he received little schooling."

JOHN McCOY was reared near Houston, and 99 years after his birth he still lived there. His memory was hazy as he talked to interviewers who visited his small shack in the rear of a Bayou City residence.

BILL McRAY, 86, was born in Milan, Texas, and interviewed at Jasper.

C. B. McRAY. Interviewers who found this Jasper native at age 76, described him as unapproachable and secretive.

SUSAN MERRITT told questioners that she was born 87 years earlier in Rusk County, Texas. She lived with her son west of Marshall.

ANNA MILLER, 85, was born in Kentucky and lived for a short time in Missouri before moving to Palo Pinto, Texas. She resided with a daughter in Fort Worth when interviewed.

MINTIE MARIA MILLER told questioners in her Galveston home of her birth 85 years earlier in Tuscaloosa, Alabama. A doctor brought her to Texas when she was very young.

WILLIAM MOORE, 82, was a native of Selma, Alabama, who moved to Mexia, Texas, during the Civil War. Interviewers found him in Dallas.

135

VAN MOORE was born on a plantation near Lynchburg, Virginia, but while a baby he moved with his master to a farm near Crosby, Texas. Eighty years later he was interviewed at his Houston home.

MANDY MORROW, a native of Georgetown, Texas, was interviewed in Fort Worth when she was 80 years old. Her fondest memories were of the years she cooked for Governor Hogg.

PATSY MOSES told questioners that she was born in Fort Bend County 74 years earlier. They interviewed her at Mart, Texas.

MARTHA PATTON came to Texas from her native Alabama when she was a baby. She lived at Goliad for most of her 91 years.

ELLEN PAYNE, 88, was born and raised in Marshall, where she still lived alone on her farm in the 1930's.

HENDERSON PERKINS hailed from near Nashville, Tennessee, but came to Centerville, Texas, before the Civil War. Interviewers found him living at age 85 in Fort Worth.

ELLEN POLK showed only a little gray hair at the temples and forehead despite her 83 years. Interviewers who met the Gonzales County, Texas, native in San Antonio also noted that her eyesight was still excellent.

BETTY POWERS, 80, was born in Harrison County, Texas. She complained to questioners who visited her in Fort Worth that her memory had failed during the preceding five years.

ALLEN PRICE told interviewers of his birth in a covered wagon 75 years earlier. He lived in Mart during the 1930's.

JOHN PRICE, about 80, born in Morgan City, Louisiana, came to Texas in 1861. He and his wife, who had recently suffered a paralytic stroke, had a small home and well-cared-for yard when interviewers found them.

LAFAYETTE PRICE didn't know his age, but he was apparently very old. The native of Wilcox County, Alabama, lived in Louisiana for a time before coming to Texas just after the Civil War. He was interviewed at Beaumont.

A. C. PRUITT, 76, was a native of St. Martinsville, Louisiana, who moved to Snowball, Texas, during the Civil War. The small, muscular man lived in Monroe City, Texas, when interviewed.

EDA RAINS was born in Little Rock, Arkansas, in 1843 and came to Texas during the Civil War. Blind by the 1930's, she lived in Douglasville, Texas.

ELSIE REECE was born in Grimes County, Texas, in 1847. She moved to Fort Worth in 1926 to live with a daughter, who supported her with the aid of a $7 monthly pension.

WALTER RIMM, a native of San Patricio County, Texas, lived in Fort Worth when interviewers talked with him.

MARIAH ROBINSON couldn't recall her age, but she was probably 90 or older. The Georgia native moved to Texas while still a little girl and remembered several encounters with Indians. She recalled her experiences from her Meridian, Texas, home.

SUSAN ROSS, 75, was born in Magnolia Springs, Texas. Questioners who met her in Jasper learned that she still helped her daughter run a small cafe. Her features and skin color suggested to the interviewers that she might have been part Indian.

ANNIE ROW. Interviewers visiting her in Fort Worth learned that she was born on a plantation near Rusk, Texas, 86 years earlier.

GILL RUFFIN, age 100, was born in Harrison County, Texas, and interviewed at Karnack.

MARTIN RUFFIN, 83, was born near Port Caddo in Harrison County. Later he worked as a cook in hotels and cafes in Marshall until forced to retire. Interviewers found him still living in Marshall, supported by a $12 monthly pension and help from the Red Cross.

FLORENCE RUFFINS' age was unknown, but she apparently was not born until during or after the Civil War. She lived in Fort Worth when the interview took place.

ABRAM SELLS did not know his age but thought he must be "well along" in the 80's. Born on a plantation southwest of Newton, he was interviewed at Jamestown, Texas.

CALLIE SHEPHERD grew up near Gilmer where she was born in 1852. When interviewed, she was cared for in Dallas by her son and his wife.

BETTY SIMMONS, who thought she must be 100 or older, was stolen from an Alabama plantation while still a baby and taken to Texas. Her memoirs were recorded in Beaumont.

BEN SIMPSON, 90, was born in Norcross, Georgia and brought to Texas by his owner before the Civil War. Questioners found him living in Madisonville, Texas, on a small old age pension.

JAMES W. SMITH, 77, a retired Baptist minister, told interviewers that he was too young to have worked as a slave. He retired from preaching in 1931 and moved to Fort Worth, where he told of his early experiences.

JOHN SNEED. Although unaware of when or exactly where he was born, Sneed said he was almost grown when freedom came. He had spent most of his life in the Austin area where he was interviewed.

YACH STRINGFELLOW, 90, was born near Brenham and lived in Waco when questioners talked to him. His memory was poor concerning recent events, but he vividly described life as a slave.

J. W. TERRILL, a native of DeSoto Parish, Louisiana, thought he was about 100 years old. He recalled having come to Texas as a slave when interviewed at Madisonville, Texas.

BILL THOMAS, 88, and his wife ELLEN, 81, lived in the Old Slave Settlement near Hondo, Texas. In 1937 an interviewer reported, "they seem to be happy; their fields are tilled; a horse and cow graze near the house; a kitchen garden is under way, and several broods of baby chicks are in the yard."

SAM JONES WASHINGTON was born on a ranch along the Colorado River in Wharton County, Texas, 88 years before questioners located him in Fort Worth. He worked as a cowboy until 1905 when he began work in the Fort Worth meat packing plants. Long retired by 1937 he received a small pension and spent his time raising a few hogs and keeping a garden.

ROSE WILLIAMS, who thought she was over 90, was born on a Bell County, Texas, plantation. Interviewers found her living in Fort Worth; she had been blind for a decade.

CAROLINE WRIGHT, a native of Louisiana, was 12 years old when emancipation came. Her father moved to Texas before the Civil War and later bought more than 300 acres of land in McLennan County. She lived with her husband in Waco when interviewers recorded her narrative.

BIBLIOGRAPHY

PRIMARY SOURCES

Manuscripts

Ballinger, Diary of William Pitt. 1860, 1862—1864. Copy in Archives, University of Texas Library, Austin.

Federal Writers' Project, *Slave Narratives, A Folk History of Slavery in the United States from Interviews with Former Slaves*. Typewritten Records Prepared by the Federal Writers' Project, Washington, D. C., 1941. Rare Book Collection, Library of Congress, Washington, D. C.

Fellows, George, Papers. Rosenberg Library, Galveston, Texas.

Huling, Thomas B., Papers. Archives, University of Texas Library.

Morgan, James, Papers. Rosenberg Library.

Perry, James Franklin, Stephen Samuel Perry, Sr., and James Franklin Perry, Jr., Papers. Archives, University of Texas Library.

Texas File, Correspondence Pertaining to Ex-Slave Studies, Records of the Federal Writers' Project, Works Progress Administration, Record Group 69, National Archives, Washington, D. C.

Williams, Austin May, Papers. Rosenberg Library.

Williams, Samuel May, Papers. Rosenberg Library.

Government Documents

Committee on Slaves and Slavery, Texas House of Representatives. *A Report and Treatise. Slavery and the Slavery Agitation*. Austin: John Marshall & Co., State Printers, 1857.

The War of the Rebellion: A Compilation of the Official Records of the Union and Confederate Armies. Washington: Government Printing Office, 1880—1901. 130 vols.

Newspapers

Campaign Chronicle. Nacogdoches. 1859.
Daily Civilian. Galveston. 1860.
Morning Star. Houston. 1841, 1843—1845.
Northern Standard. Clarksville. 1850.
San Antonio News. 1864.
Southern Intelligencer. Austin. 1858.
Standard. Clarksville. 1856, 1861.
Telegraph and Texas Register. Houston. 1843, 1846.
Texas State Gazette. Austin. 1857.
Texas Monument. LaGrange. 1852.
Texas Republican. Marshall. 1849, 1861, 1865.
Texas State Times. Austin. 1855—1857.
Weekly Independent. Belton. 1857.
Weekly Journal. Galveston. 1853.

Barker, Eugene C. Ed. *The Austin Papers*. Washington and Austin: American Historical Association and the University of Texas Press, 1924—1926. 3 vols.

Barker, Nancy Nichols. Ed. *The French Legation in Texas*. Austin: Texas State Historical Association, 1971. Vol. I.

Botkin, B. A. Ed. *Lay My Burden Down: A Folk History of Slavery*. Chicago: University of Chicago Press, 1945.

Drew, Benjamin. *The Refugee: A North-Side View of Slavery*. Reading, Mass.: Addison-Wesley Pub. Co., 1969 reprint.

Egypt, Ophelia Settle, J. Masuoka, and Charles S. Johnson. *Unwritten History of Slavery: Autobiographical Accounts of Negro Ex-Slaves*. Nashville: Fiske University Social Documents Series, No. 1, 1945.

Featherstonhaugh, George William. *Excursion Through the Slave States from Washington on the Potomac to the Frontier of Mexico*. London: John Murray, 1844. 2 vols.

Ford, John S. *Rip Ford's Texas*. Ed. by Stephen B. Oates. Austin: University of Texas Press, 1963.

Fremantle, Arthur James Lyon. *The Fremantle Diary; Being the Journal of Lieutenant Colonel Arthur James Lyon Fremantle, Coldstream Guards, on His Three Months in the Southern States*. Ed. by Walter Lord. Boston: Little, Brown & Co., 1954.

Gaillardet, Frédéric. *Sketches of Early Texas and Louisiana*. Trans. and intro. by James L. Shepherd III. Austin: University of Texas Press, 1966.

Gray, William F. *From Virginia to Texas, 1835: Diary of Col. Wm. F. Gray, Giving Details of His Journey to Texas and Return in 1835—1836 and Second Journey to Texas in 1837*. Houston: Fletcher Young Pub. Co., 1965.

Gulick, Charles Adams, Jr., and others. Eds. *The Papers of Mirabeau Buonaparte Lamar*. Austin: A. C. Baldwin & Sons, 1921—1927. 6 vols.

Hollon, W. Eugene, and Ruth Lapham Butler. Eds. *William Bollaert's Texas*. Norman: University of Oklahoma Press, 1956.

Houzeau, J. C. *La terreur blanche au Texas, et mon évasion*. Bruxelles: Ve. Parent & Fils, Editeurs, 1862.

Kennedy, William. *Texas: The Rise, Progress, and Prospects of the Republic of Texas*. London: R. Hastings, 1841. 2 vols.

Lubbock, Francis Richard. *Six Decades in Texas, or Memoirs of Francis Richard Lubbock, Governor of Texas in War-Time, 1861—63*. Ed. by C. W. Raines. Austin: Ben C. Jones & Co., Printers, 1900.

McDonald, Archie P. Ed. *Hurrah for Texas! The Diary of Adolphus Sterne, 1838—1851*. Waco: The Texian Press, 1969.

Marcy, Randolph Barnes. *Thirty Years of Army Life on the Border*. New York: Harper & Bros., Pub., 1866.

Olmsted, Frederick Law. *A Journey in the Back Country*. New York: Mason Bros., 1860.

————. *A Journey Through Texas; or, a Saddle-Trip on the Southwestern Frontier*. New York; Dix, Edwards & Co., 1857.

Osofsky, Gilbert. Ed. *Puttin' on Ole Massa: The Slave Narratives of Henry Bibb, William Wells Brown, and Solomon Northup*. New York: Harper & Row, Pubs., 1969.

Reagan, John H. *Memoirs, with Special Reference to Secession and the Civil War*. Ed. by Walter F. McCaleb. New York: Neale Pub. Co., 1906.

140

Sheridan, Francis C. *Galveston Island, or a Few Months off the Coast of Texas: The Journal of Francis C. Sheridan, 1839–1840.* Ed. by Willis W. Pratt. Austin: University of Texas Press, 1954.

Williams, Ameila W., and Eugene C. Barker. Eds. *The Writings of Sam Houston, 1813–1863.* Austin: University of Texas Press, 1938–1943. 8 vols.

Yetman, Norman R. Ed. *Life Under the "Peculiar Institution": Selections from the Slave Narratives Collection.* New York: Holt, Rinehart and Winston, Inc., 1970.

Articles

Almonte, Juan N. "Statistical Report on Texas," trans. by C. E. Castañeda, *Southwestern Historical Quarterly* XXVIII (Jan., 1925), 177–221.

[Brown, John Henry.] "African Slavery," *The Texas Almanac for 1858.* Galveston: The "News," 1857.

Cade, John B. "Out of the Mouths of Ex-Slaves," *Journal of Negro History*, XX (July, 1935), 294–337.

Harris, Mrs. Dilue. "The Reminiscences of Mrs. Dilue Harris, I," *Quarterly of the Texas State Historical Association*, IV (Oct., 1900), 85–127.

"Notes and Fragments," *Quarterly of the Texas State Historical Association*, IX (April, 1906), 285.

SECONDARY SOURCES

Manuscripts

Littlejohn, R. P. "The Negro of the South," included with interview conducted at Marshall, Texas, Sept. 12, 1887. Transcript P-O 39, H. H. Bancroft Collection, Bancroft Library, University of California, Berkeley.

Books

Barker, Eugene C. *The Life of Stephen F. Austin, Founder of Texas, 1793–1836.* Austin: University of Texas Press, 1969 reprint.

———. *Mexico and Texas, 1821–1835.* Dallas: P. L. Turner Co., 1928.

Connor, Seymour V. *Texas, a History.* New York: Thomas Y. Crowell Co., 1971.

Diccionario Porrúa de historia y geografía de México. 2nd ed., México: Editorial Porrúa, 1965.

Dillon, Merton L. *Benjamin Lundy and the Struggle for Negro Freedom.* Urbana: University of Illinois Press, 1966.

Elkins, Stanley M. *Slavery: A Problem in American Institutional and Intellectual Life.* New York: Grosset & Dunlap Universal Library, 1963.

Fornell, Earl Wesley. *The Galveston Era: The Texas Crescent on the Eve of Secession.* Austin: University of Texas Press, 1961.

Genovese, Eugene D. *The Political Economy of Slavery: Studies in the Economy and Society of the Slave South.* New York: Vintage Books, 1967.

Hogan, William Ransom. *The Texas Republic: A Social and Economic History.* Austin: University of Texas Press, 1969 reprint.

Jackson, Lynnell. *True Witnesses: A Check List of Newspapers, 1845–1861.* Austin: Department of Journalism, University of Texas at Austin, 1971.

Lathrop, Barnes F. *Migration Into East Texas, 1835–1860: A Study from the United States Census.* Austin: Texas State Historical Association, 1949.

141

Lomax, John A. *Adventures of a Ballad Hunter*. New York: The Macmillan Co., 1947.

McDonald, William F. *Federal Relief Administration and the Arts*. Columbus, Ohio: Ohio State University Press, 1969.

Phillips, Ulrich B. *American Negro Slavery: A Survey of the Supply, Employment and Control of Negro Labor as Determined by the Plantation Regime*. Baton Rouge: Louisiana State University Press, 1969 reprint.

Richardson, Rupert N. *Texas: The Lone Star State*. 2nd ed. rev., Englewood Cliffs, N. J.: Prentice-Hall, Inc., 1958.

————, Ernest Wallace, and Adrian N. Anderson. *Texas: The Lone Star State*. 3rd ed. rev., Englewood Cliffs, N. J.: Prentice-Hall, Inc., 1970.

Stampp, Kenneth M. *The Peculiar Institution: Slavery in the Ante-Bellum South*. New York: Vintage Books, 1956.

Waller, John L. *Colossal Hamilton of Texas: A Biography of Andrew Jackson Hamilton, Militant Unionist and Reconstruction Governor*. El Paso: Texas Western Press, University of Texas at El Paso, 1968.

Webb, Walter P., and H. Bailey Carroll. Eds. *The Handbook of Texas*. Austin: Texas State Historical Association, 1952. 2 vols.

Articles

Addington, Wendell G. "Slave Insurrections in Texas," *Journal of Negro History*, XXXV (Oct., 1950), 408—434.

Barker, Eugene C. "The African Slave Trade in Texas," *Quarterly of the Texas State Historical Association*, VI (Oct., 1902), 145—158.

————. "The Influence of Slavery on the Colonization of Texas," *Mississippi Valley Historical Review*, XI (June, 1924), 3—36.

Bertleth, Rosa Groce, "Jared Ellison Groce," *Southwestern Historical Quarterly*, XX (Apr., 1917), 358—368.

Bugbee, Lester G. "Slavery in Early Texas," I and II, *Political Science Quarterly*, XIII (Sept. and Dec., 1898), 389—410, 648—668.

Bullock, Henry Allen. "A Hidden Passage in the Slave Regime," in James C. Curtis and Lewis L. Gould. Eds. *The Black Experience in America; Selected Essays*. Austin. University of Texas Press, 1970.

Curlee, Abigail. "The History of a Texas Slave Plantation, 1861—63," *Southwestern Historical Quarterly*, XXVI (Oct., 1922), 79—127.

Fornell, Earl W. "Agitation in Texas for Reopening the Slave Trade," *Southwestern Historical Quarterly*, LX (Oct., 1956), 245—259.

Howren, Alleine. "Causes and Origin of the Decree of April 6, 1830," *Southwestern Historical Quarterly*, XVI (Apr., 1913), 378—422.

Porter, Kenneth Wiggins. "Negroes and Indians on the Texas Frontier, 1831—1876," *Journal of Negro History*, XLI (July and Oct., 1956), 185—214, 285—310.

Schoen, Harold, "The Free Negro in the Republic of Texas, *Southwestern Historical Quarterly*, XXXIX (Apr., 1936), 292—308; XL (July, 1936), 26—34; (Oct., 1936), 85—113; (Jan., 1937),169—199; (Apr., 1937), 267—289; XLI (July, 1937), 83—108.

Somers, Dale A. "James P. Newcomb: The Making of a Radical," *Southwestern Historical Quarterly*, LXXII (Apr., 1969), 449—469.

Tyler, Ronnie C. "The Callahan Expedition of 1855: Indians or Negroes?" *Southwestern Historical Quarterly*, LXX (Apr., 1967), 574—585.

_____ , "Fugitive Slaves in Mexico," *Journal of Negro History*, LVII (Jan., 1972), 1—120.

White, William W. "The Texas Slave Insurrection of 1860," *Southwestern Historical Quarterly*, LII (Jan., 1949), 259—285.

Winningham, Mrs. David. "Sam Houston and Slavery," *Texana*, III (Summer, 1965), 93—104.

Woolfolk, George R. "Cotton Capitalism and Slave Labor in Texas," *Southwestern Social Science Quarterly*, XXXVII (June, 1956), 43—52.

Dissertations

Curlee, Abigail. "A Study of Texas Slave Plantations, 1822 to 1865." Unpublished Ph.D. Dissertation, University of Texas, Austin, 1932.

Kifer, Allen F. "The Negro Under the New Deal, 1933—1941." Unpublished Ph.D. Dissertation, University of Wisconsin, 1961.